Juggling Balls for Beginners

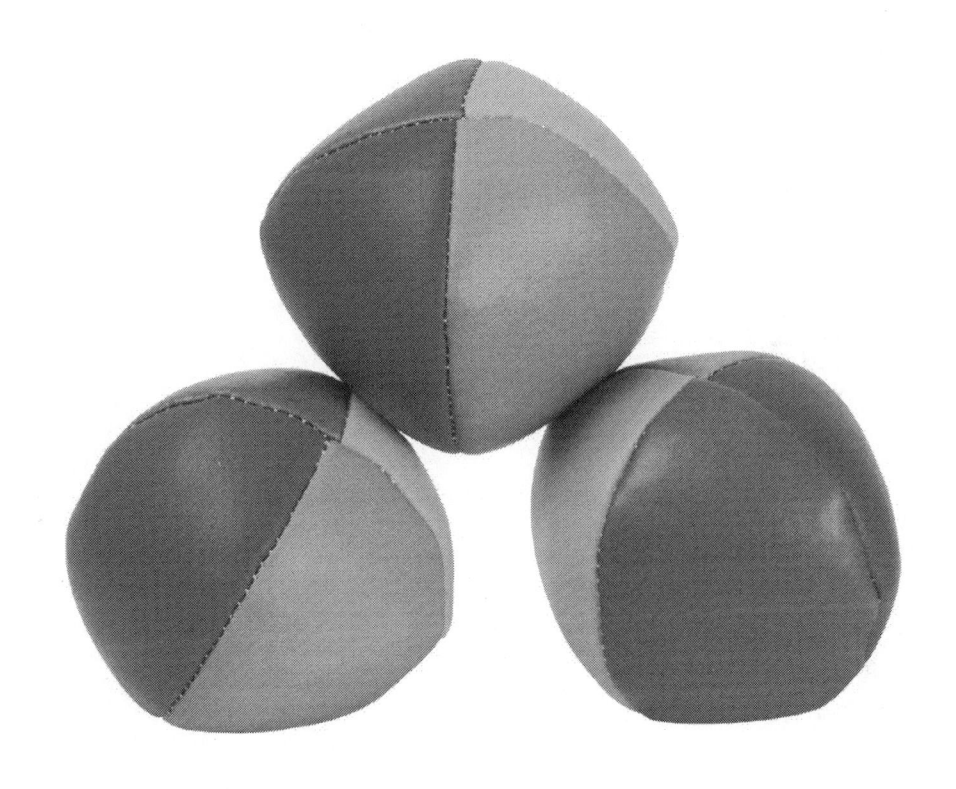

Benjamin Wise
Publishing

Juggling Balls for Beginners

ALL RIGHTS RESERVED

No part of this book may be reproduces in any form - photocoping, electronic audio recording or otherwise without written permission of a author.

Introduction

Welcome to "Juggling Balls for Beginners," a delightful journey into the world of juggling! This book is your first step into an exciting hobby that combines skill, coordination, and a touch of whimsy. Whether you are a complete novice with no experience or someone who has always been fascinated by the art of juggling but never knew where to start, this book is designed for you.

Juggling is more than just a circus act; it's a form of expression, a brain-boosting exercise, and a great way to impress your friends and family. Throughout this book, we'll guide you through the basics of juggling with balls, starting with fundamental concepts and gradually moving to more advanced techniques. Our step-by-step instructions are easy to follow, and each chapter is filled with illustrations and tips to ensure your learning process is both effective and fun.

In the following pages, you will discover the history of juggling, understand its benefits for your mind and body, and, most importantly, learn the techniques to juggle three balls with confidence. We have also included a section on troubleshooting common problems and tips to enhance your practice sessions.

So, grab your juggling balls, and let's embark on this exciting journey together. Prepare to amaze yourself with what you can achieve with a little practice and a lot of enthusiasm!

The history of juggling is rich and diverse, spanning several millennia and various cultures across the globe. Its origins and development reflect the changing social, cultural, and entertainment landscapes throughout human history.

Juggling's earliest known records date back to around 2000 B.C. in Egypt. Artifacts and wall paintings, particularly in an ancient Egyptian tomb from the Middle Kingdom (1994-1781 B.C.), depict figures juggling balls. This indicates that juggling was practiced as a form of entertainment or skill demonstration in ancient Egyptian society. Additionally, evidence of juggling has been found in other ancient civilizations, including Greece, Rome, and China, highlighting its widespread appeal and practice in early human history.

In the Roman Empire, juggling was a recognized and admired skill. Various Roman writers and poets, like Martial, described jugglers' performances, illustrating their dexterity and skill. For example, the juggler Agathinus was known for his extraordinary shield manipulation routine. There are also accounts of Roman citizens like Ursus, who played with a glass ball, and Rabbi Shimon ben Gamliel, who could juggle eight torches without them touching. This period also saw juggling acts involving knife throwing, as observed by the Church father Chrysostom in Antioch around AD 450.

During the Middle Ages, juggling was one of the skills performed by entertainers and jesters. It was a common feature in courts and public spaces. Illuminated manuscripts and other historical records from this period provide evidence of jugglers' presence in medieval European society. For instance, William the Conqueror's minstrel, Taillefer, is recorded as having performed a juggling trick at the Battle of Hastings in 1066

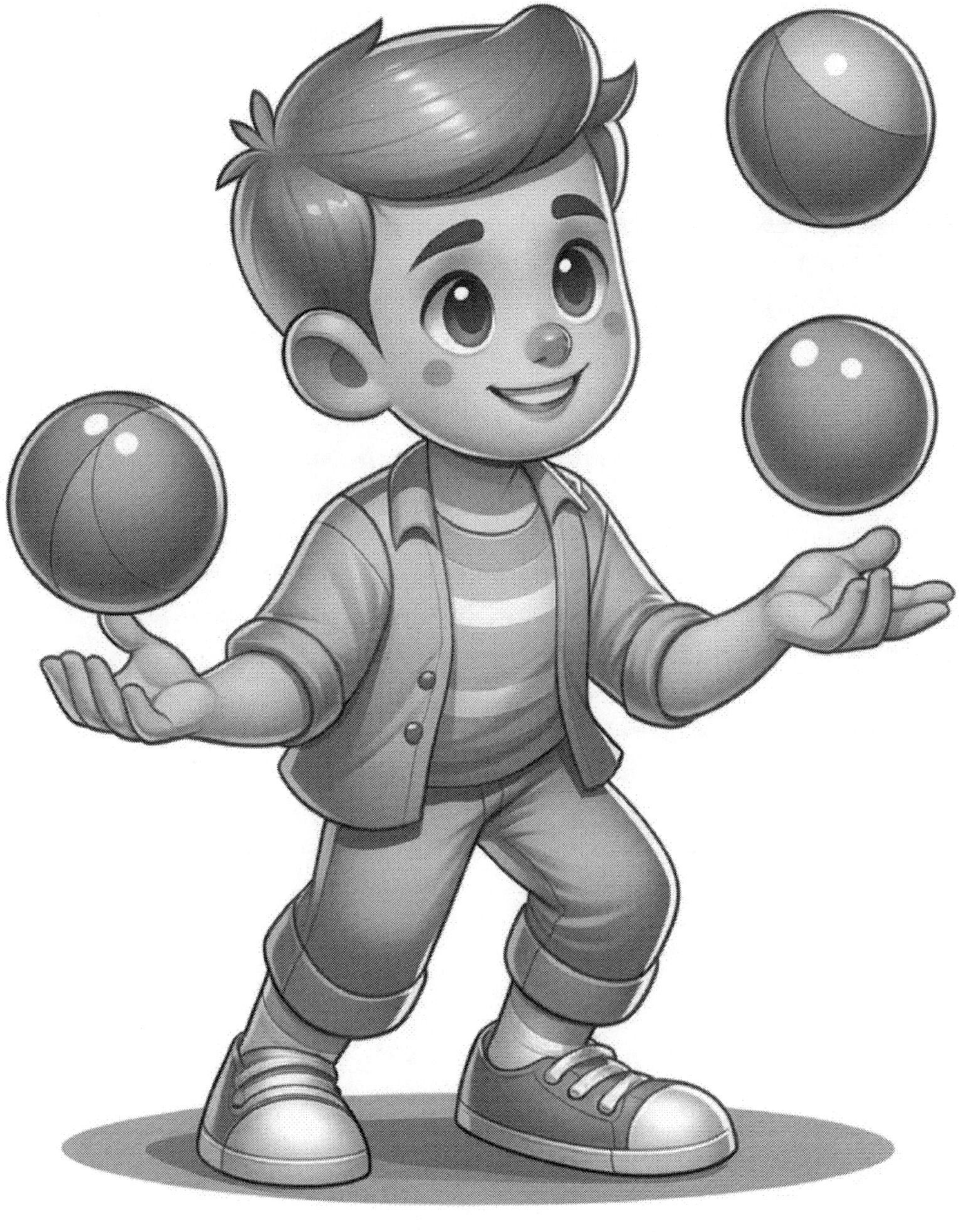

Juggling continued to evolve and grow in popularity during the Renaissance and later periods. It became a common act in street performances and was often combined with music, storytelling, and other forms of entertainment. The derivation of the word "juggle" itself comes from the Middle English word "joggled," meaning to perform or entertain.

In the modern era, especially from the 18th century onwards, juggling became a staple in circuses and vaudeville shows. It was no longer just an individual skill but became part of larger entertainment acts. Jugglers began to be featured in circuses in the 1760s, and by the late 1880s, they were integral to the emerging style of vaudeville entertainment. With the advent of movies and television, the nature of juggling as an entertainment medium evolved, adapting to new audiences and formats
.
Throughout its history, juggling has been more than just an entertainment art; it has been a skill that required immense dexterity and was often associated with physical and mental agility. From ancient Egyptian tombs to modern-day circuses and street performances, juggling has maintained its appeal, continually evolving and adapting to the tastes and cultures of different eras.

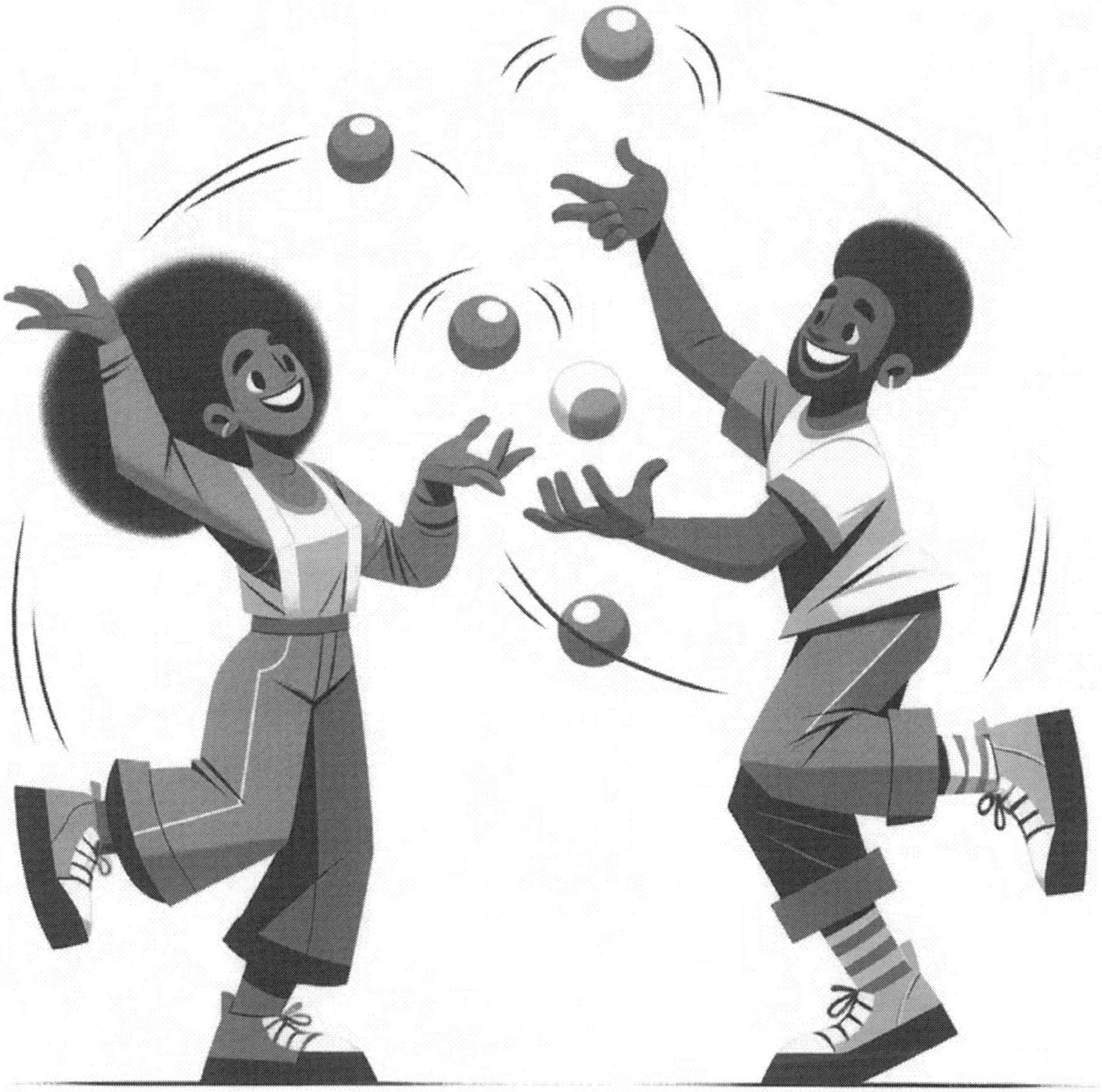

Juggling, throughout its history, has often reflected the social and cultural contexts of the times. In ancient civilizations, it was possibly seen as a skill of the elite or as part of religious or ceremonial events. In the Roman Empire, it was a form of entertainment that even high-ranking officials and citizens enjoyed. However, with the fall of the Roman Empire and the onset of the Middle Ages, the perception towards jugglers shifted. They were sometimes seen as vagabonds or associated with witchcraft, indicating a societal change in how entertainment and skills like juggling were perceived

The Renaissance marked a revival of juggling, integrating it more into the arts. Jugglers started to be seen more positively, often performing for royalty and being part of the entourage of musicians, poets, and storytellers. This era also saw a blend of juggling with other forms of art, indicating a shift towards a more holistic approach to entertainment. The skill was no longer just about the act of juggling but also about how it could enhance other art forms.

The transition from the Renaissance to modern times saw significant changes in the way juggling was presented and perceived. The development of circuses and later vaudeville theatres provided new platforms for jugglers. The circus environment, in particular, allowed for more dramatic and grandiose juggling acts, often involving multiple objects or dangerous items like fire and knives. This period also saw the professionalization of juggling as entertainers started to be formally recognized and paid for their skills.

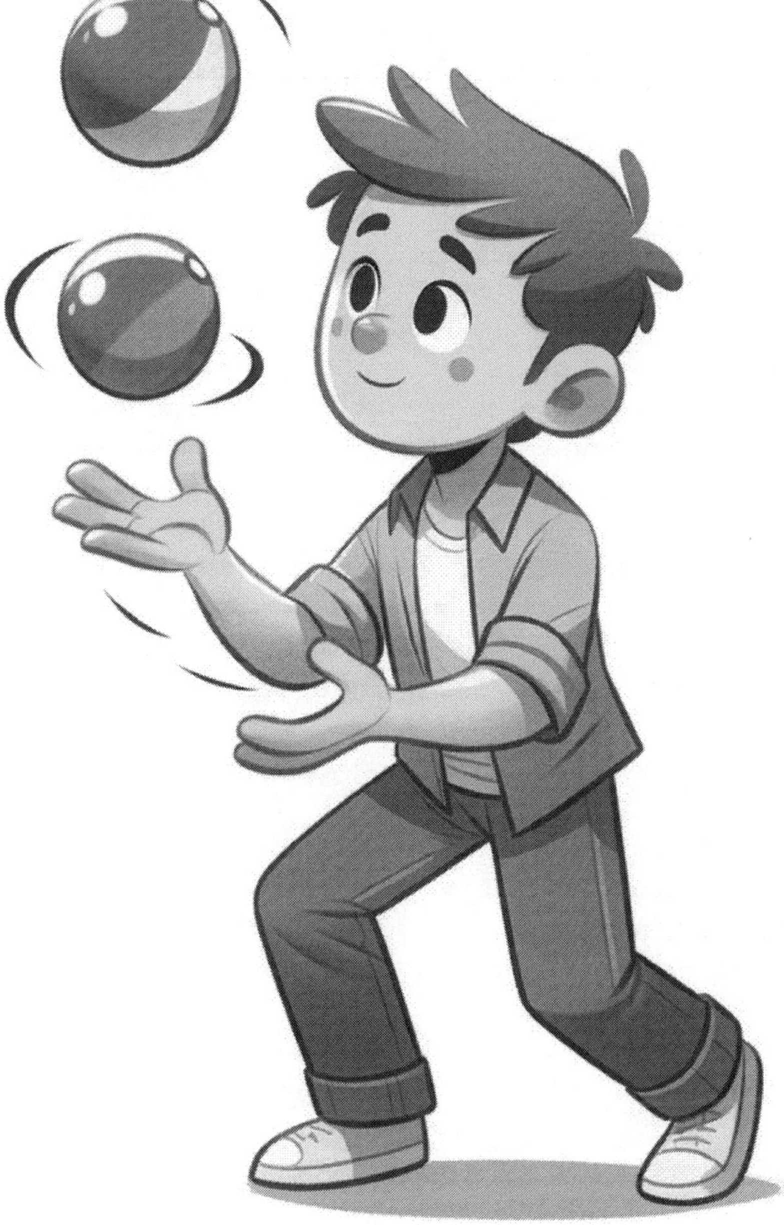

In the 18th and 19th centuries, juggling became a popular act in circuses across Europe and the United States. Philip Astley, often considered the father of the modern circus, included jugglers in his shows from as early as 1768. The United States saw its first circus jugglers in 1793. This period also marked the beginning of jugglers providing entertainment in theaters during set changes and intermissions, indicating a broader acceptance and demand for this art form.

By the late 19th century, juggling was a key component of Vaudeville, a style of variety entertainment popular in the United States and Canada. This period saw jugglers sharing the stage with comedians, musicians, and other performers, showcasing a wide array of juggling styles and techniques. The decline of Vaudeville with the rise of cinema and television led to a shift in how jugglers performed, with many adapting to the new media or finding niches in live entertainment venues like nightclubs and variety shows.

In the contemporary era, juggling continues to be a popular form of entertainment and skill. It has branched out into various styles and forms, with jugglers often combining traditional techniques with modern technology and artistic expression. The growth of hobbyist communities, juggling conventions, and online platforms has also helped to keep the art form vibrant and evolving.

Juggling's journey from an ancient skill to a modern entertainment form illustrates its adaptability and enduring appeal. Its history not only reflects changes in entertainment styles but also broader social and cultural shifts. From being an elite skill in ancient times to a popular form of entertainment in the modern world, juggling has consistently been a fascinating aspect of human creativity and skill.

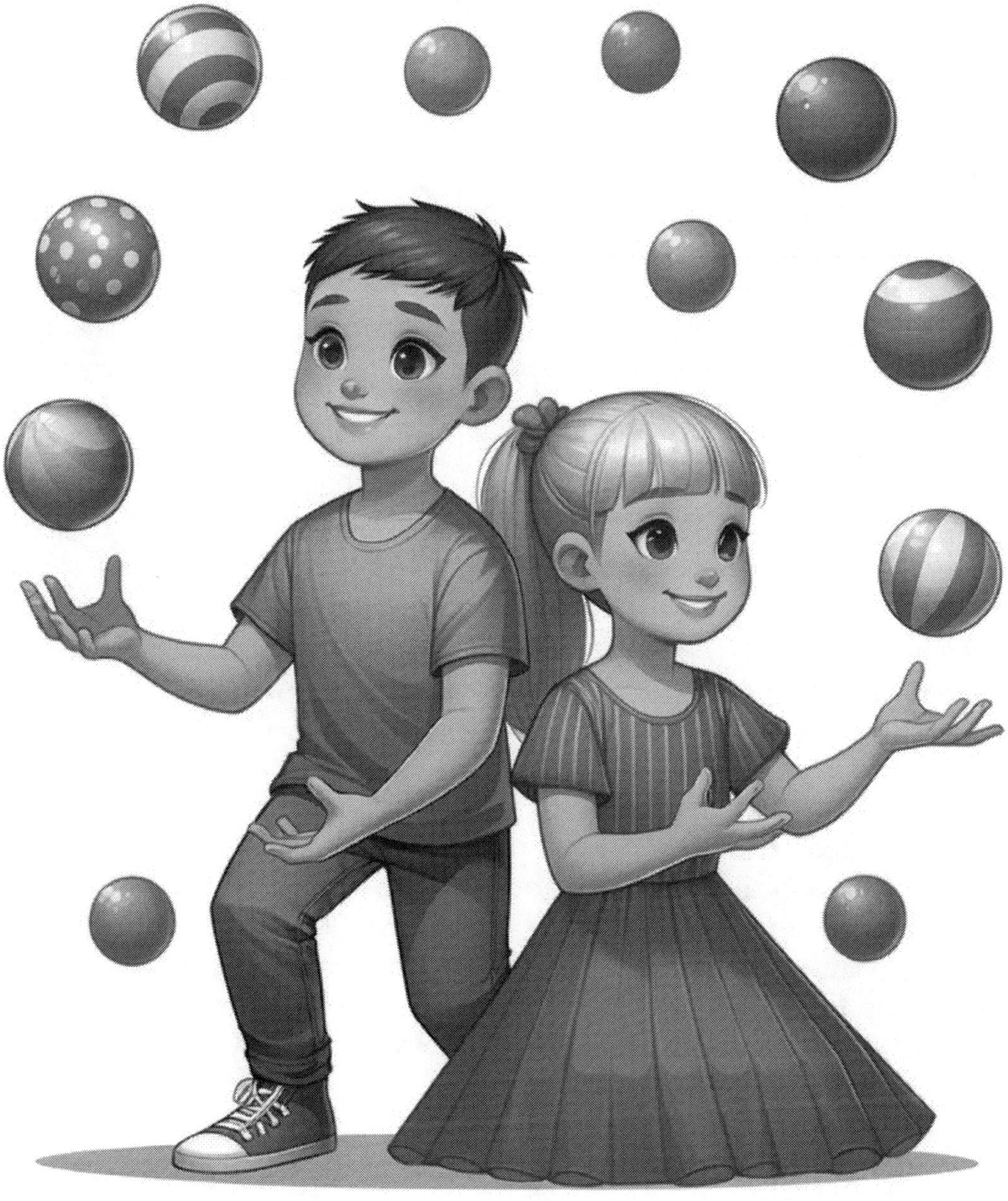

As exploration and trade expanded from the 16th century onwards, so too did the exchange of cultural practices, including juggling. European explorers and traders encountered juggling traditions in Asia, Africa, and the Americas, often bringing these influences back to Europe. Similarly, European juggling techniques and styles spread to other continents. This cultural exchange enriched the art of juggling globally, leading to a fusion of styles and techniques.

The Industrial Revolution and subsequent technological advancements had a significant impact on juggling. The availability of new materials allowed for the creation of innovative juggling props. Rubber, plastics, and lightweight metals led to the development of juggling clubs, rings, and other apparatus that were easier to handle and allowed for more complex and varied routines. This period also saw the invention of juggling machines, which showcased mechanical precision in mimicking human juggling skills, demonstrating the intersection of technology and art.

The 20th century witnessed a renaissance in juggling, partly driven by the rise of mass media. Jugglers began to appear in films, television shows, and later in online videos, reaching a broader audience than ever before. This exposure helped to popularize juggling and introduced it to new generations. The art form also saw significant evolution in technique, with jugglers pushing the boundaries of what was considered possible. Records for the most objects juggled, the longest duration, and the most complex patterns were continually broken and re-established.

Juggling is not just an art; it is also a science. The latter part of the 20th century and the early 21st century saw increased interest in the physics and mathematics of juggling.

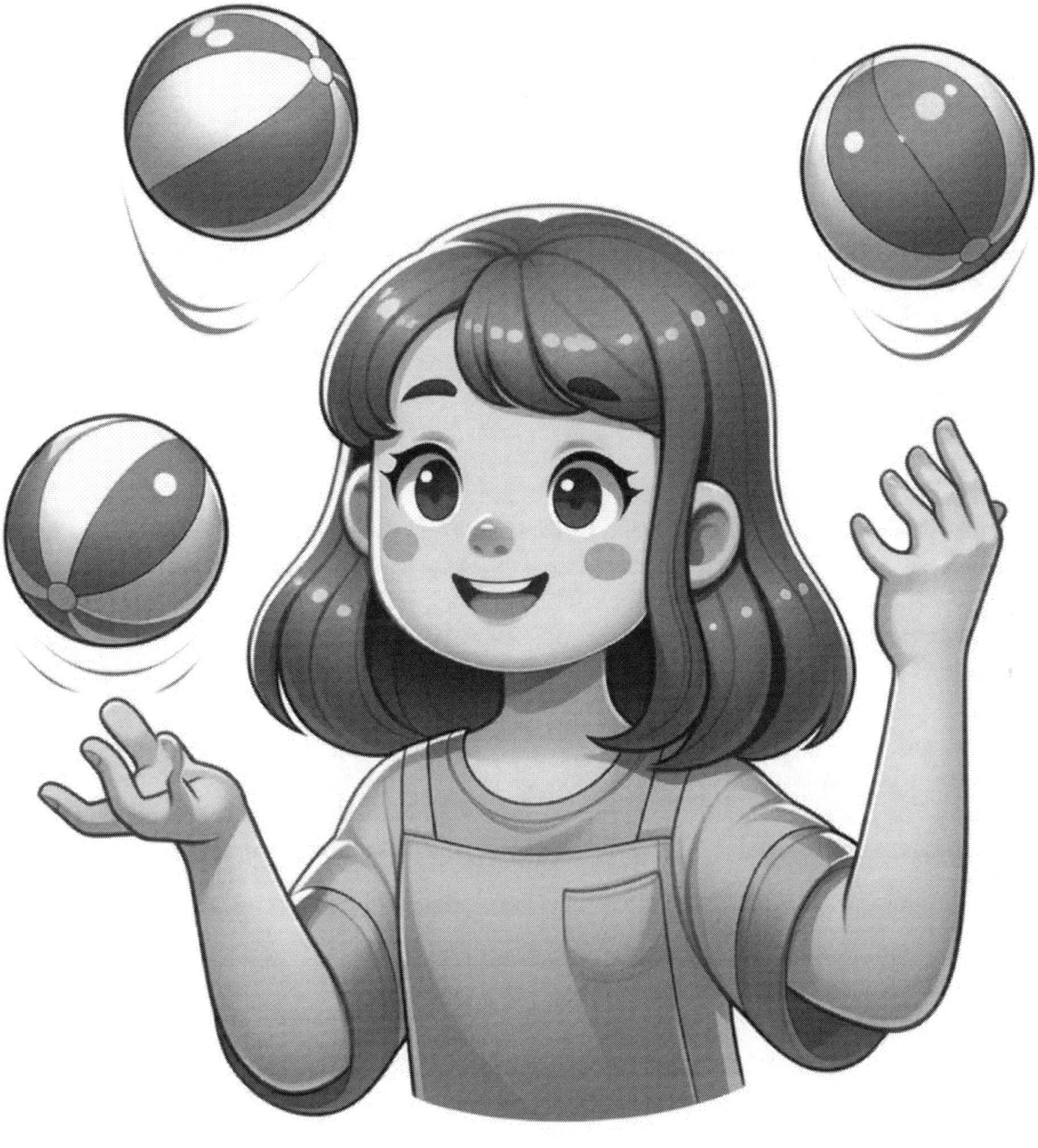

In popular culture, jugglers have often been portrayed in various roles, from the comic and whimsical to the skillful and awe-inspiring. Juggling has featured in movies, television shows, and theater productions, sometimes as a central theme and other times as a captivating interlude. The image of the juggler has evolved from the medieval court jester to a modern performer who combines skill, creativity, and entertainment.

The late 20th and early 21st centuries have seen the rise of juggling communities and festivals around the world. These gatherings, such as the European Juggling Convention and the International Jugglers' Association Festival, bring together amateurs and professionals to share skills, perform, and celebrate the art of juggling. They provide a platform for learning, collaboration, and showcasing new talents and innovations in the field.

Juggling's journey through history reveals it as a dynamic and ever-evolving art form. From its ancient origins to its current status as a globally practiced and appreciated skill, juggling continues to fascinate and entertain. Its ability to blend art, science, and physical dexterity makes it a unique and enduring element of human culture and creativity.

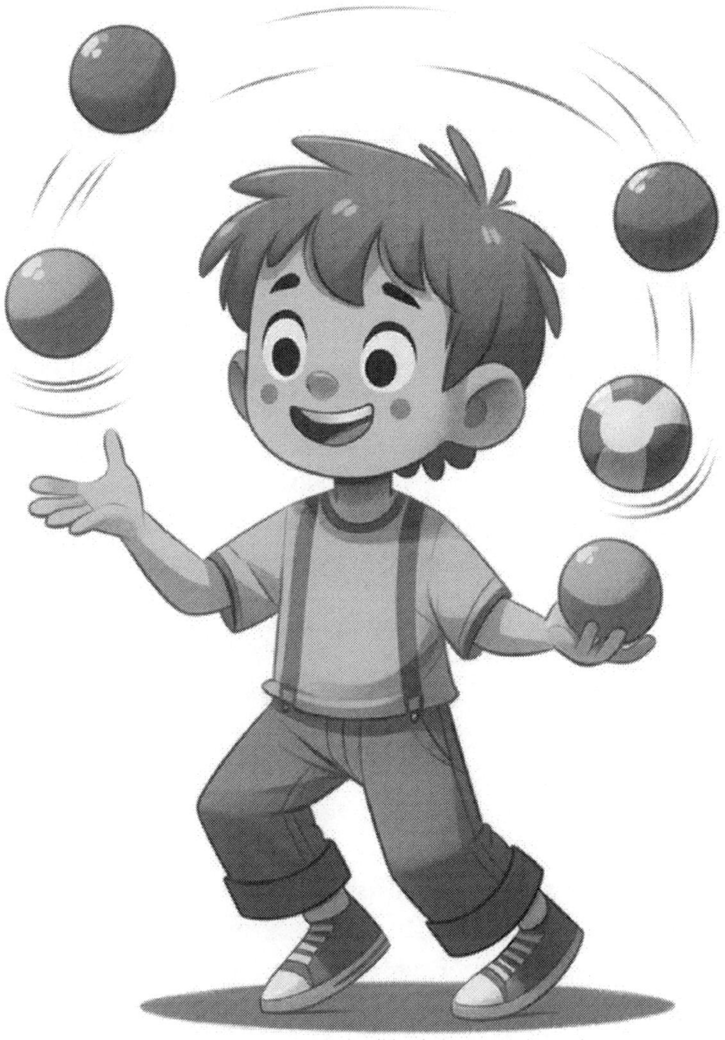

The 20th century saw a significant diversification in juggling styles. Traditional forms of juggling involving balls, clubs, and rings were complemented by innovative techniques and props. Contact juggling, which involves rolling objects over the hands and body, became popular. Other forms like diabolo, devil sticks, and poi spinning were integrated into juggling acts, demonstrating the art's adaptability and diversity.

Advancements in media technology profoundly impacted how juggling was learned, shared, and developed. The advent of the internet and video-sharing platforms in the late 20th and early 21st centuries opened up new avenues for jugglers to connect, share techniques, and showcase their skills to a global audience. Instructional videos and online tutorials became vital tools for aspiring jugglers, democratizing access to learning resources.

The competitive aspect of juggling gained prominence with the organization of juggling championships and competitions. These events not only showcased skill and creativity but also fostered a spirit of community among jugglers. Competitions often featured categories like numbers juggling, endurance, and team juggling, highlighting the diverse skill sets within the community.

Educational institutions began to recognize the benefits of juggling in physical education and cognitive development. Studies suggested that juggling could improve hand-eye coordination, and concentration, and even aid in brain development. Consequently, juggling workshops and programs were introduced in schools and educational settings, promoting it as a beneficial and fun activity.

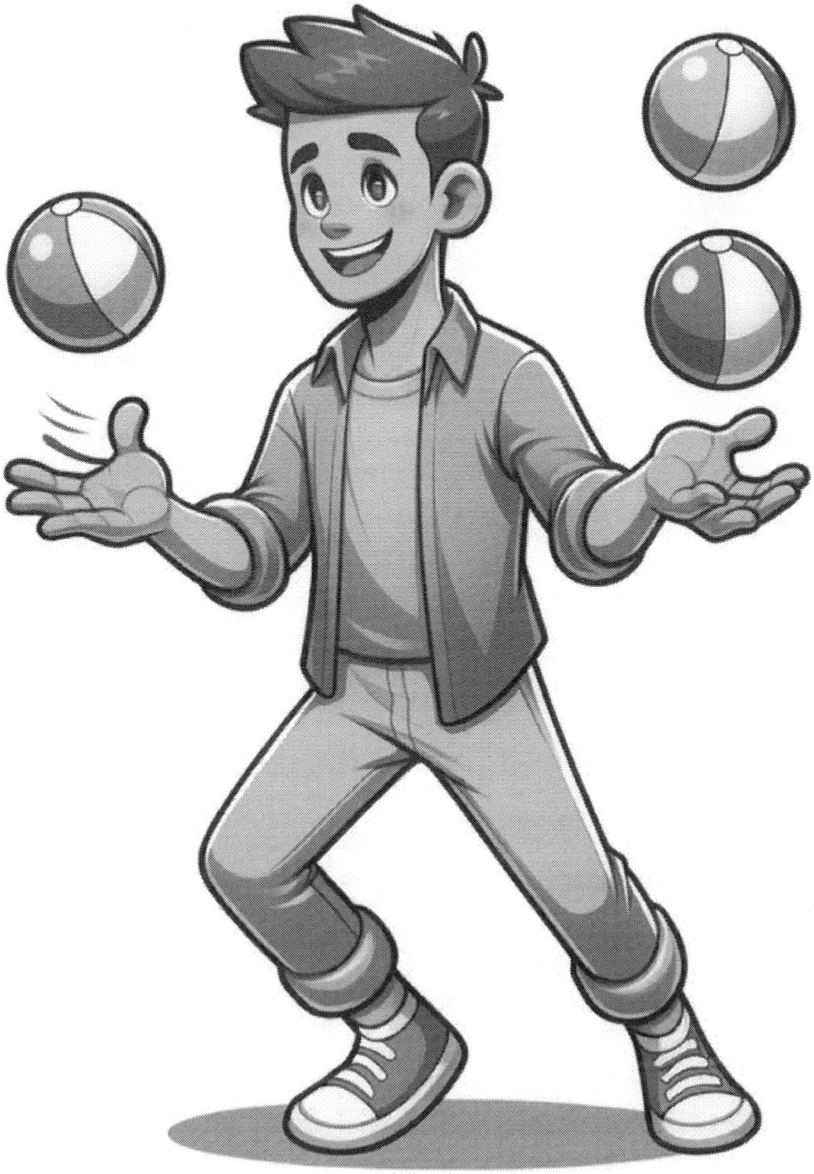

Juggling also found a place in social and therapeutic contexts. Workshops and programs using juggling as a tool for social engagement, team-building, and even therapy began to emerge. Its ability to foster a sense of achievement, improve mental health, and build community ties highlighted its role beyond entertainment.

Looking towards the future, juggling continues to evolve with technological advancements and cultural shifts. The incorporation of digital technology, such as LED-equipped juggling props and virtual reality, points to new directions for this ancient art form. The global juggling community, connected and vibrant, continues to innovate and push the boundaries of what juggling can be.

In summary, the modern era of juggling is characterized by its rich diversity, integration with technology, educational value, and evolving cultural significance. As an art form that balances skill, creativity, and physical prowess, juggling remains a dynamic and fascinating element of global cultural heritage.

In the 21st century, juggling has firmly established itself in contemporary culture. It is not only a form of entertainment but also a means of artistic expression and personal development. Juggling festivals and conventions continue to be popular, attracting enthusiasts from all over the world. These events serve as platforms for sharing knowledge, showcasing talent and fostering a sense of community among jugglers.

Technological advancements have significantly influenced modern juggling. The use of LED and programmable props has introduced a new visual dimension to juggling performances, particularly in dark environments.

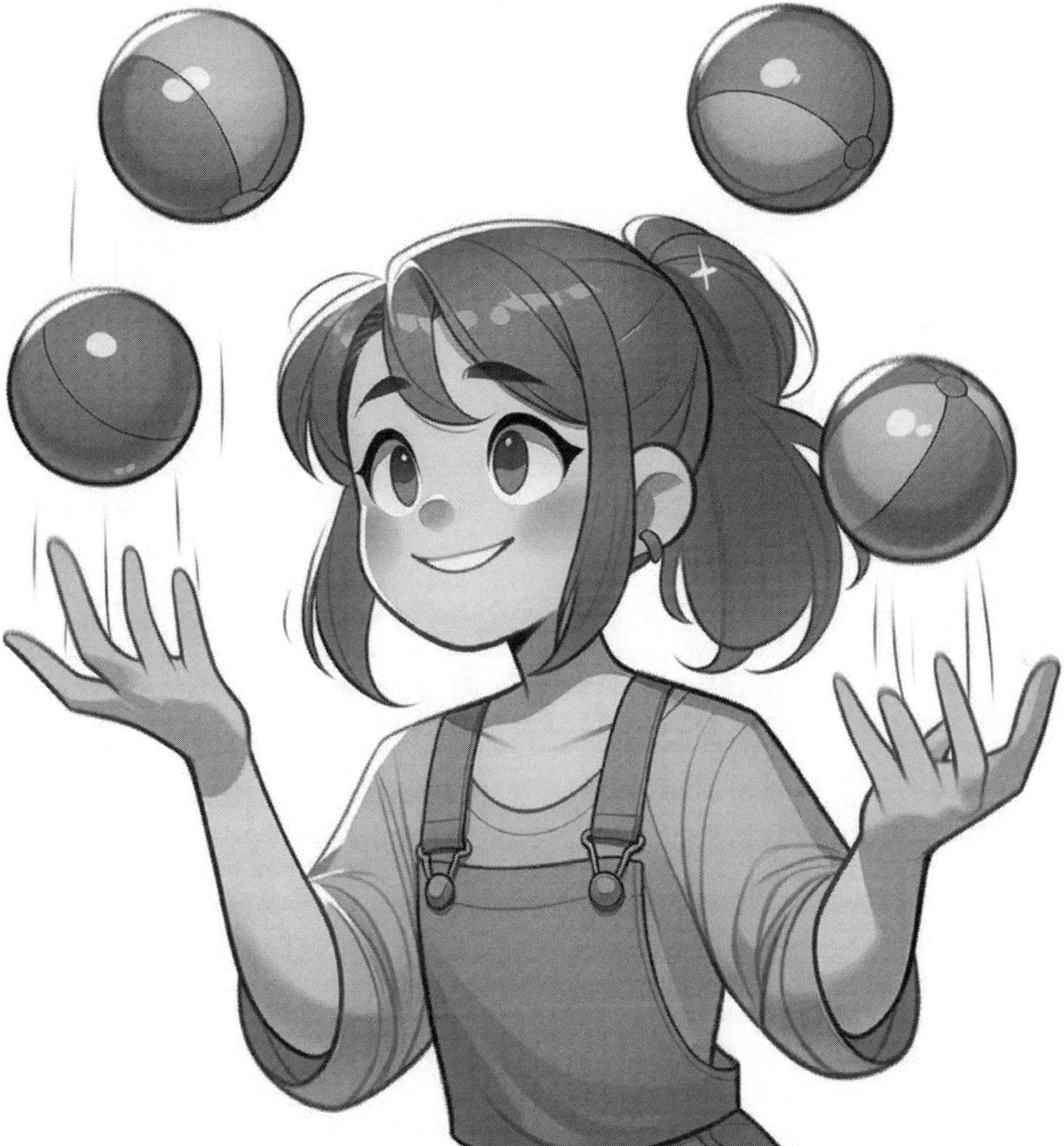

Juggling's role in education has expanded, with numerous studies underscoring its benefits in enhancing cognitive skills, coordination, and concentration. Schools and educational programs increasingly incorporate juggling into their curricula, recognizing its potential to improve motor skills and provide a fun, engaging way for students to learn.

The therapeutic benefits of juggling are gaining recognition in the fields of physical and mental health. Juggling is used in physical therapy to improve coordination and fine motor skills. In mental health, it serves as a stress reliever and a tool for mindfulness, helping individuals to focus and find mental clarity.

In the entertainment industry, juggling continues to evolve. Modern jugglers often blend traditional techniques with elements of comedy, drama, and storytelling, creating multifaceted performances. The incorporation of juggling into theater, dance, and even music videos demonstrates its versatility and appeal as a performance art.

Social media has played a crucial role in popularizing juggling among younger generations. Platforms like YouTube, Instagram, and TikTok allow jugglers to share their skills, connect with audiences worldwide, and inspire others to take up juggling. This has led to the emergence of new juggling stars and influencers who have brought fresh perspectives to the art.

Looking ahead, the future of juggling appears vibrant and full of potential. The ongoing fusion of juggling with technology, its increasing recognition as a beneficial activity for health and education, and its ever-evolving artistic expressions suggest that juggling will continue to captivate and inspire people across the world.

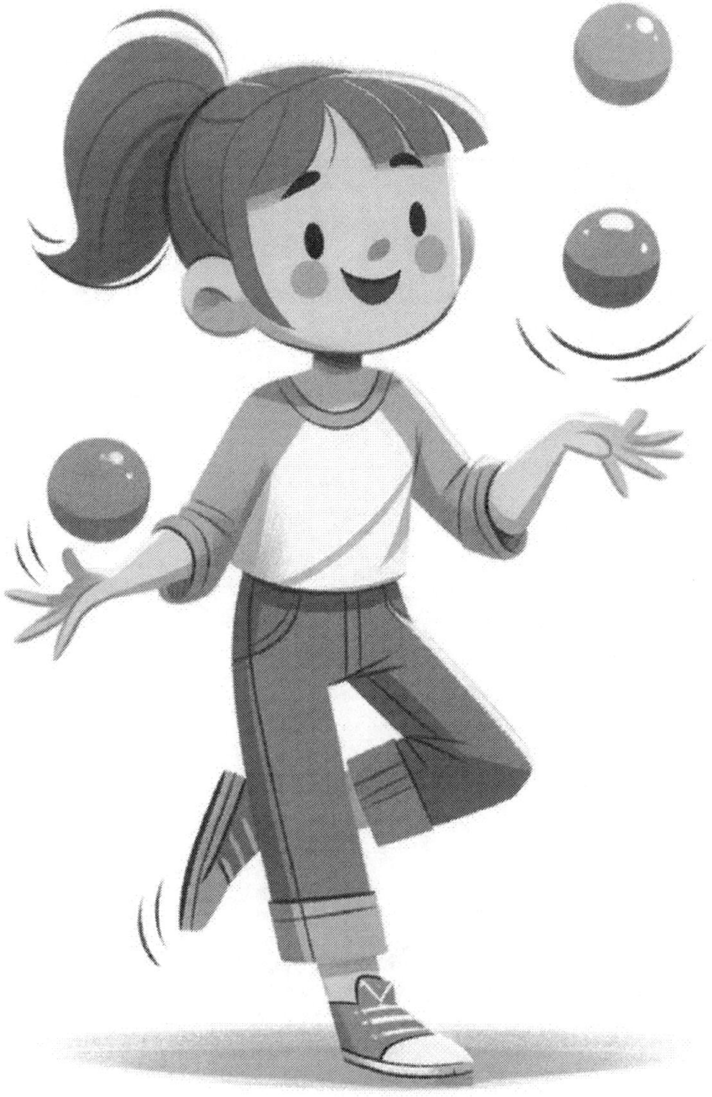

Preparing for Juggling

To prepare for juggling, begin by assuming a proper posture: stand with your shoulders aligned with your feet and elbows bent at 90 degrees. Start with one ball, throwing it back and forth between your hands in a gentle arc above eye level. Focus on consistency in your throws and catches, aiming for the ball to peak at the same height each time. Practice this with your eyes closed to improve consistency.

Once comfortable with one ball, introduce a second ball. Throw the second ball underneath the first when it peaks, aiming for both balls to reach the same height. Add a third ball once you've mastered two balls, starting with two balls in your dominant hand and one in the other. Throw the third ball before the second ball comes down, and practice until you can make 5 throws and 5 catches.

Regarding juggling balls for beginners, consider size, weight, and material. Smaller, lightweight balls are recommended for beginners, with a size of around 2.5 inches and a weight that's easy to handle. Soft bean bag balls are ideal as they don't roll away when dropped. Two recommended sets for beginners are the Taylor Tries Signature Juggling Ball Set and the Klutz 3 Ball Juggling Kit. These sets offer good size, and weight, and are designed for easy handling and durability.

To further prepare for juggling, it's important to create a conducive environment and use the right tools. Choose a space with enough room to move freely, with no obstructions. Good lighting is crucial for visibility. As for equipment, select juggling balls or beanbags that are comfortable to hold and won't roll away when dropped. Also, wear comfortable clothing that doesn't restrict movement.

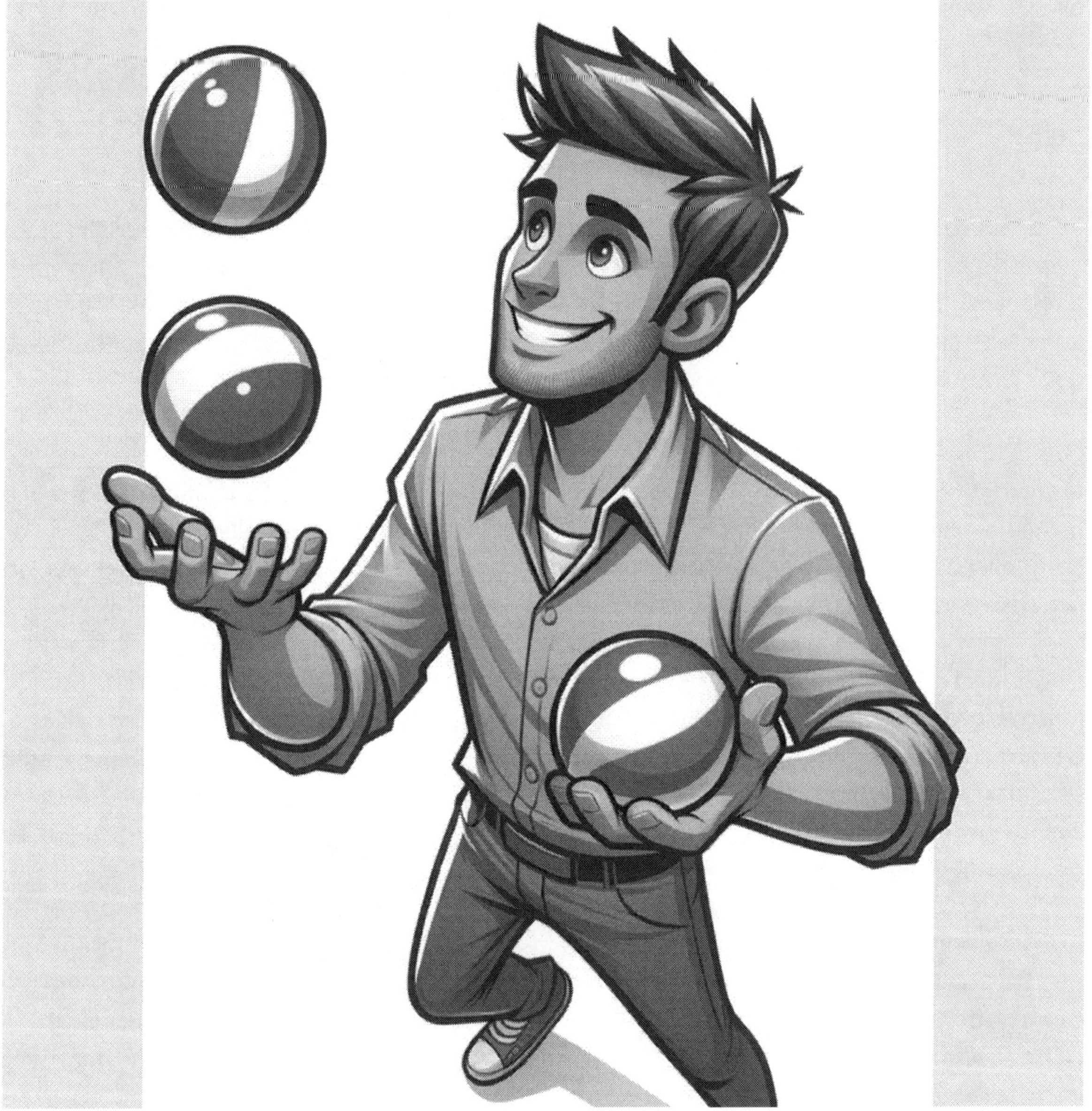

Proper hand stretching is crucial for juggling, as it helps prevent injuries and improves flexibility and dexterity. Here's a simple routine to stretch your hands and fingers effectively:

Wrist Rotations: Extend your arms in front of you with your palms facing down. Gently rotate your wrists ten times in a clockwise direction, then ten times counterclockwise. This warms up the wrists, which are heavily involved in juggling.

Finger Stretches: Extend your hand and spread your fingers as wide as possible. Hold this position for a few seconds, then relax. Repeat this five times for each hand. This stretch improves the range of motion and flexibility in your fingers.

Thumb Stretch: Hold one hand out with the palm facing you. Gently pull back on the thumb with the other hand until you feel a comfortable stretch. Hold this position for about 15-20 seconds and then switch to the other thumb.

Palm Stretch: Extend your arm in front of you with the palm facing outward and fingers pointing down. Use your other hand to gently press on the back of the stretched hand, pushing slightly towards the body, to stretch the palm and the underside of the wrist. Hold for 15-20 seconds and then switch hands.

Finger Flexion and Extension: Curl your fingers to make a fist, then release and stretch them out as far as possible. Repeat this motion smoothly for about 10-15 times. This exercise helps in maintaining the flexibility and strength of the fingers and hands.

Wrist Flexor Stretch: Extend one arm in front of you at shoulder height. Keep your elbow straight and fingers pointing up. With your other hand, gently press down on the fingers of the extended hand to stretch the wrist flexors. Hold for 15-20 seconds, then switch hands.

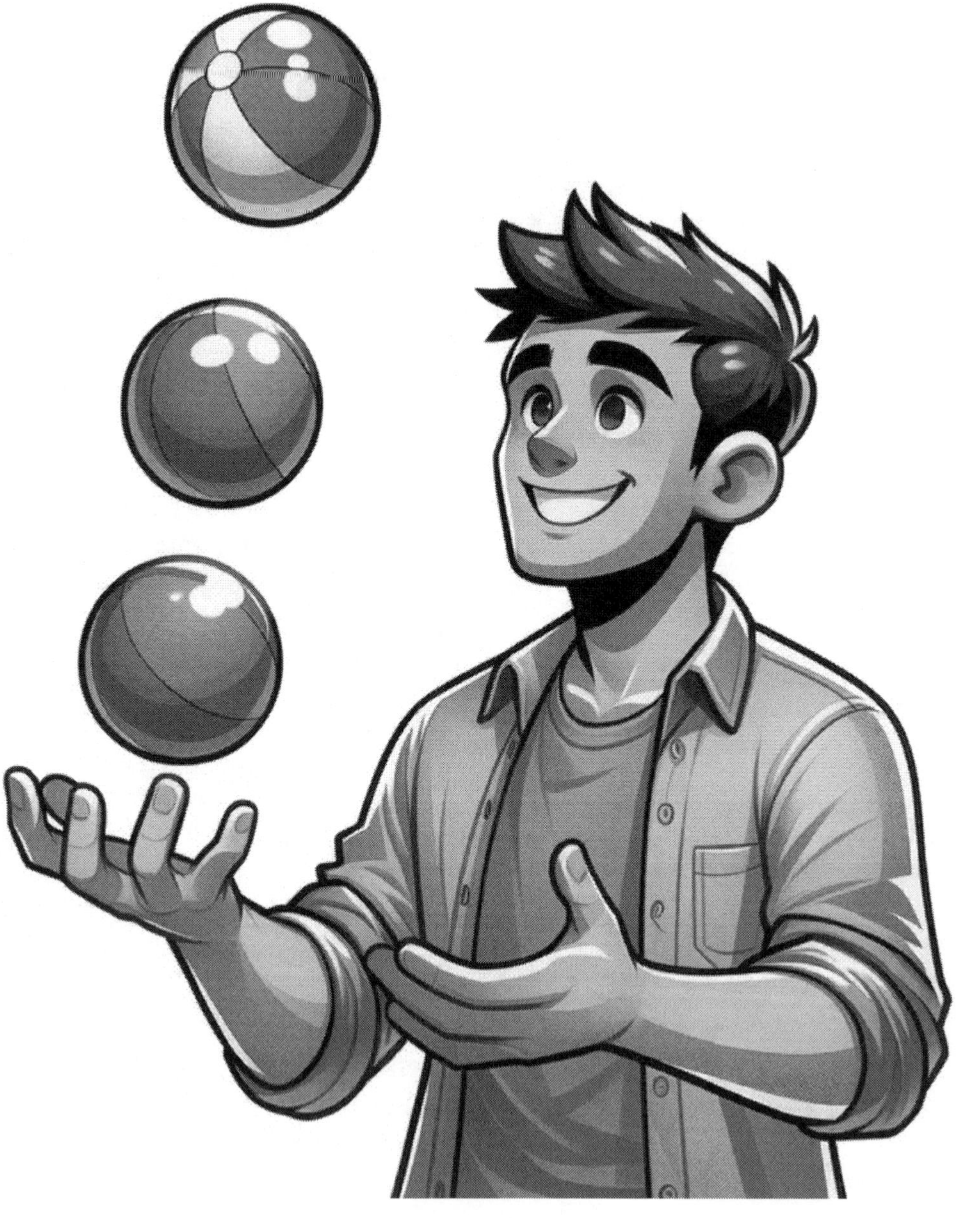

Understanding One Ball Practice

Objective: The primary goal of One Ball Practice is to develop a consistent and controlled throw and catch rhythm, which is the cornerstone of juggling.

Technique:
Starting Position: Stand with your feet shoulder-width apart, and hold a ball in one hand.

Throwing: Toss the ball gently in an arc to about eye level or slightly higher. Aim for a spot just above and slightly in front of your opposite shoulder.

Catching: Watch the ball as it reaches the top of the arc and then descends. Catch it with your opposite hand at about waist level.

Returning: Repeat the process, this time throwing the ball back to the original hand.
  Why It's Important

Hand-Eye Coordination: This practice enhances your hand-eye coordination, a crucial skill in juggling.

Consistent Throws: It helps in mastering the art of making consistent throws

 Consistency in height, angle, and speed of throws is vital for moving on to more balls.

Timing and Rhythm: One Ball Practice develops a sense of timing and rhythm, which is necessary for juggling multiple balls.

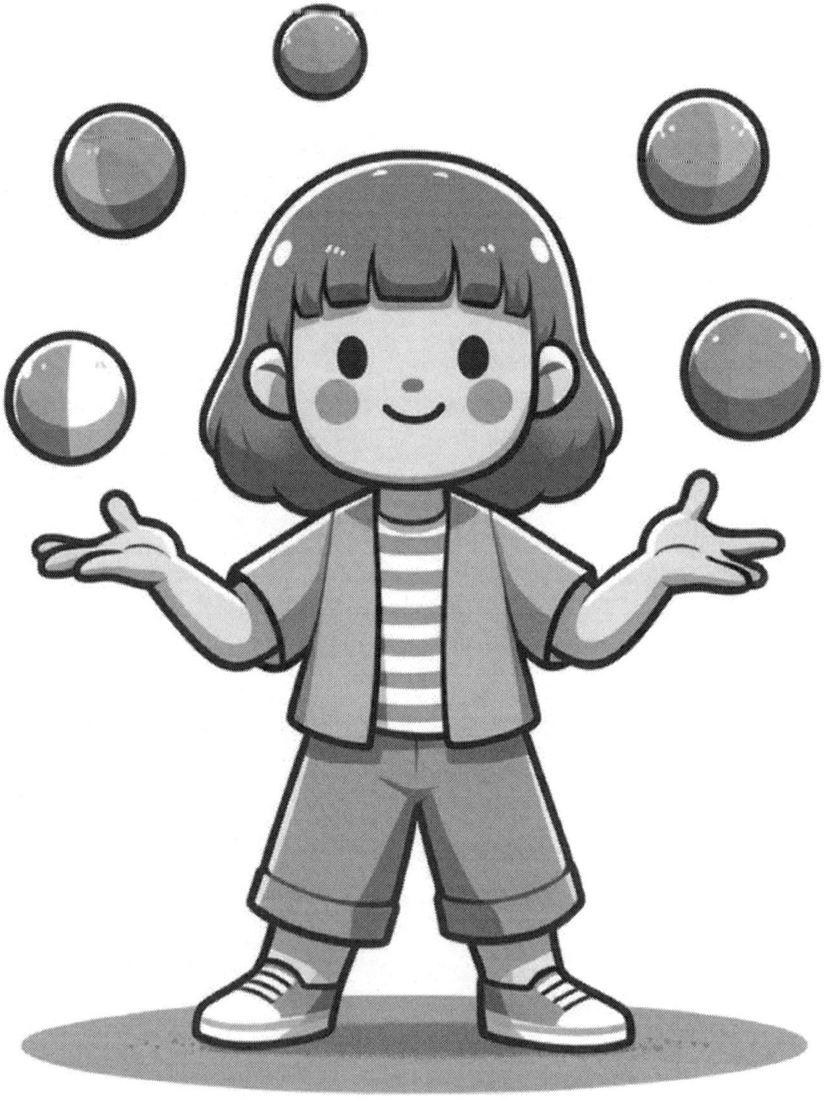

Focus: It teaches you to focus on the apex of the throw, an important aspect of juggling. Watching the highest point of the throw allows better anticipation and timing for catches and subsequent throws.

Building Confidence: For beginners, successfully throwing and catching one ball provides a confidence boost and a foundation to build upon.

Tips for Practice

Relax: Keep your movements relaxed. Tension in your arms or shoulders can make your throws erratic.

Consistent Arc: Aim for a consistent arc in each throw.

Steady Pace: Start with a slow and steady pace. Speed can come later.

Repetition: Repetition is key. The more you practice, the more natural the movements will become.

One Ball Practice is a simple yet effective way to begin your juggling journey. It lays the groundwork for more advanced techniques and helps build the muscle memory needed for juggling multiple balls.

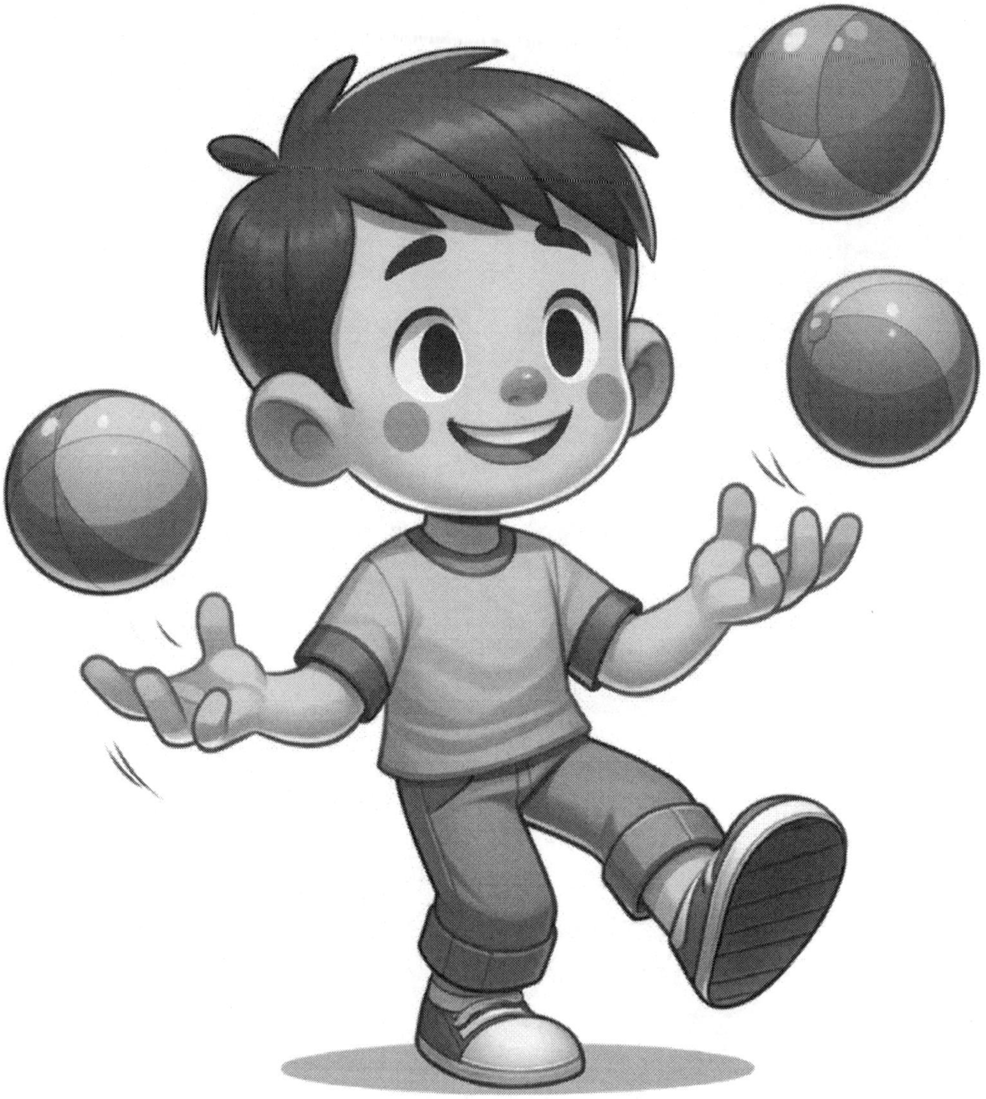

Juggling two balls in one hand is a skill that forms an integral part of many juggling routines, and it's a great stepping stone towards more complex patterns. Here's an overview of how to practice and master this technique:

Understanding the Technique
Objective: The goal is to keep two balls moving in a circular pattern within one hand, using a scooping motion.

Technique:
Starting Position: Hold two balls in one hand. For beginners, it's often easier to start with the dominant hand.

First Throw: Toss the first ball from the pinky side of your hand towards the thumb side, aiming for a peak just above eye level.

Second Throw: As the first ball reaches its peak and begins to fall, scoop your hand underneath it and throw the second ball from the thumb side to the pinky side, following a similar arc.

Catching and Continuing: Catch the first ball with the same hand as it comes down. By this time, the second ball will be reaching its peak, ready for you to scoop and throw again.

Rhythm: The key is to maintain a steady rhythm. The throws should be even and consistent, with each ball following a similar path.

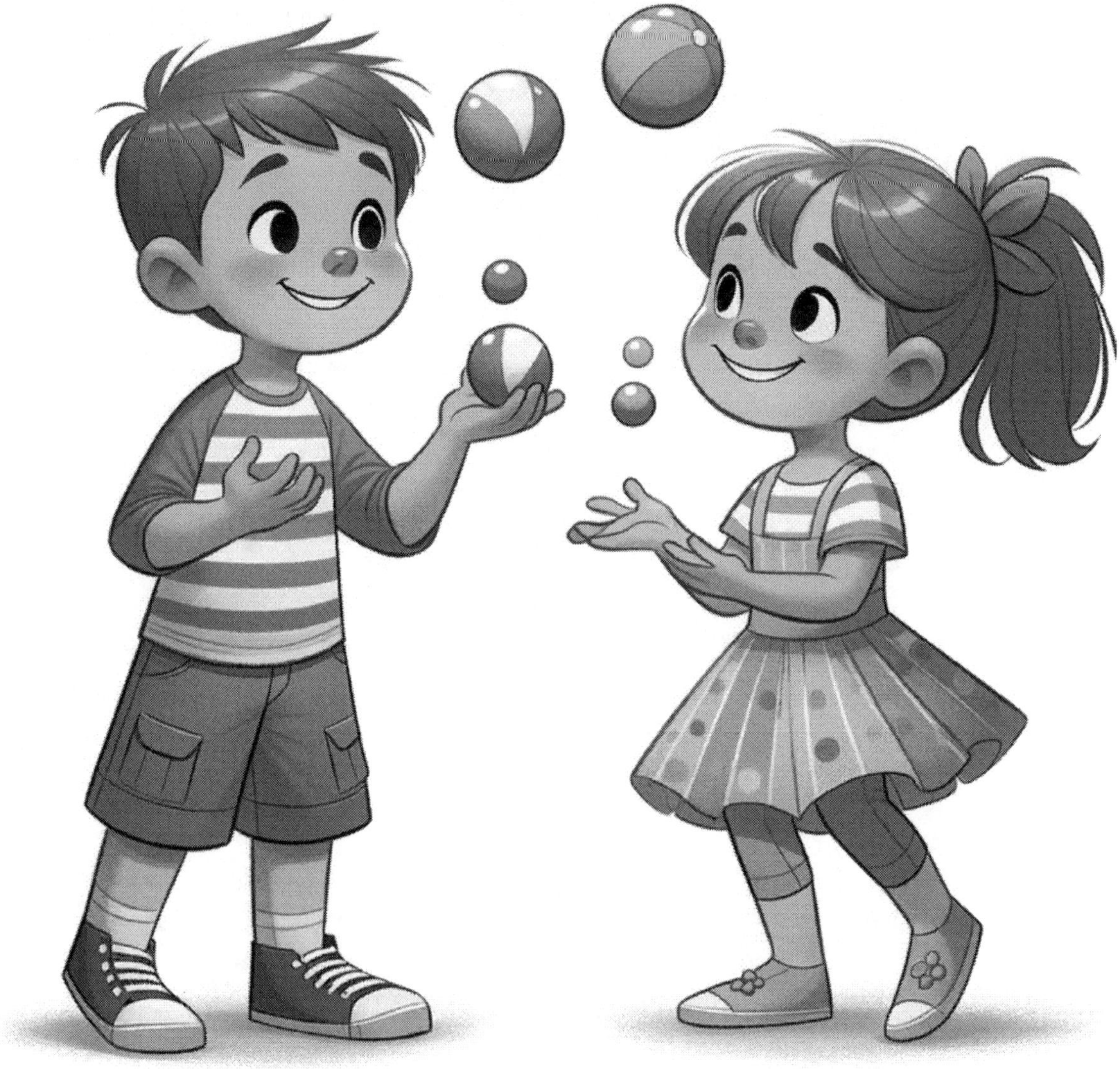

Tips for Practice

Focus on One Ball at a Time: Initially, focus on getting a consistent throw with one ball before adding the second.

Scooping Motion: Practice the scooping motion without the balls. This motion helps to keep the balls in a controlled circular pattern.

Even Height and Arc: Both balls should have a similar height and arc to maintain a consistent pattern.

Slow and Steady: Start slowly. Speed can be increased as you gain more control.
Use of Space: Try to keep the pattern tight and within a small space. Wider patterns are harder to control and can lead to more mistakes.

Practice Both Hands: While it's easier to start with your dominant hand, practicing with both hands is beneficial, especially if you want to progress to more advanced juggling patterns.

Timing: Getting the timing right between the two throws can be tricky. It might take some practice to find the rhythm that works for you.
Hand Fatigue: This technique can be tiring on the hand and wrist. Take breaks as needed.

Once comfortable with two balls in one hand, you can try alternating the pattern between both hands or incorporate it into more complex juggling routines involving more balls or different objects.

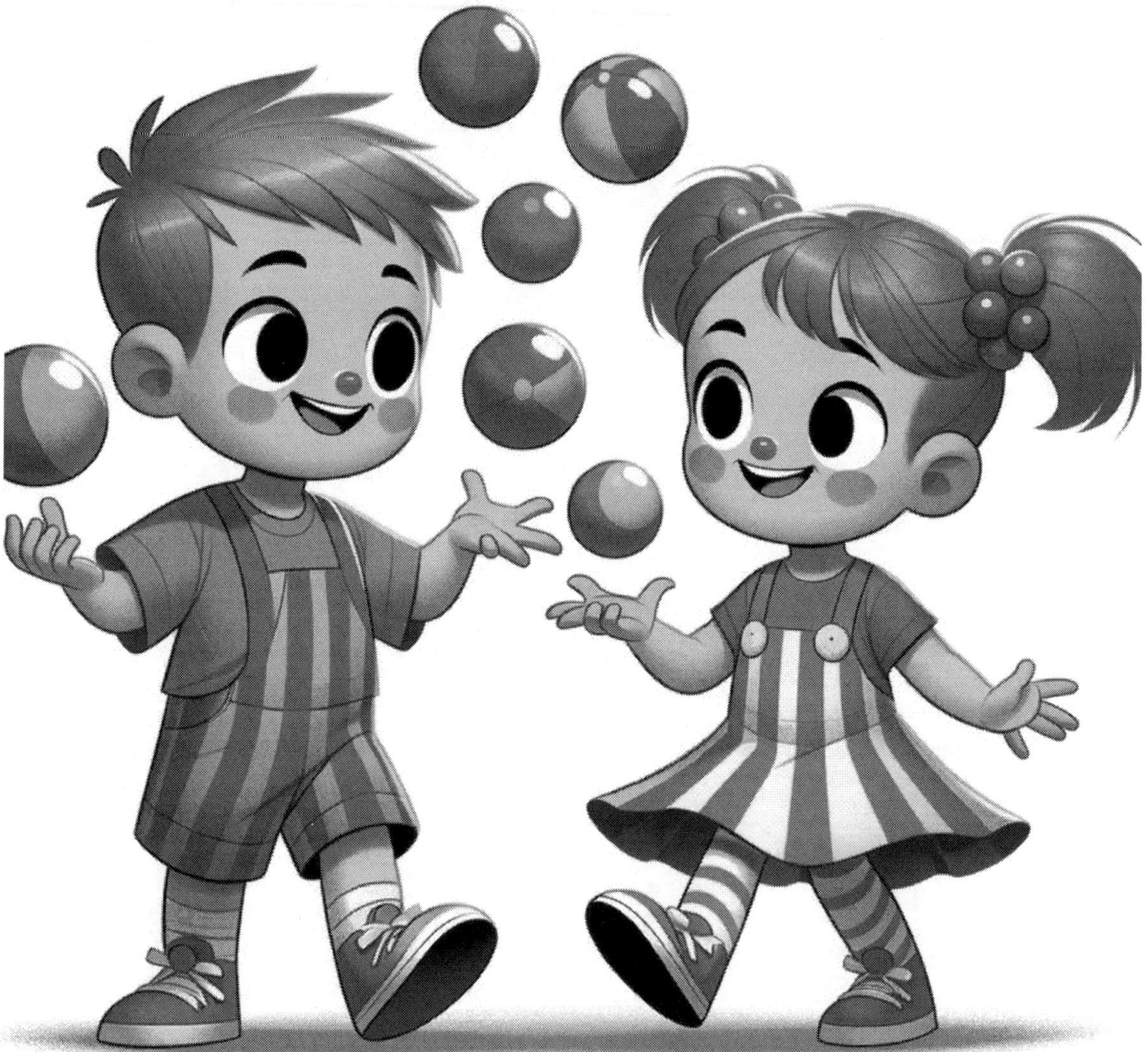

The Two Ball Exchange is a fundamental juggling pattern that is ideal for beginners. It's essentially the first step towards learning the three-ball cascade, the most basic juggling pattern. Here's how to practice the Two Ball Exchange:

Understanding the Two-ball Exchange

Objective: The aim is to get comfortable with the motion of throwing and catching two balls in an alternating pattern, which is crucial for progressing to juggling three balls.
Technique:

Starting Position: Hold one ball in each hand.

First Throw: Toss one ball (let's say from your right hand if you're right-handed) in an arc to the left hand. The peak of the arc should be just above eye level.

Second Throw: As soon as you release the first ball, and before catching it with the left hand, throw the second ball from your left hand to your right hand in a similar arc.

Catching: Catch the first ball in your left hand and then catch the second ball in your right hand.

Repeat: Continue this pattern, alternating throws between each hand.

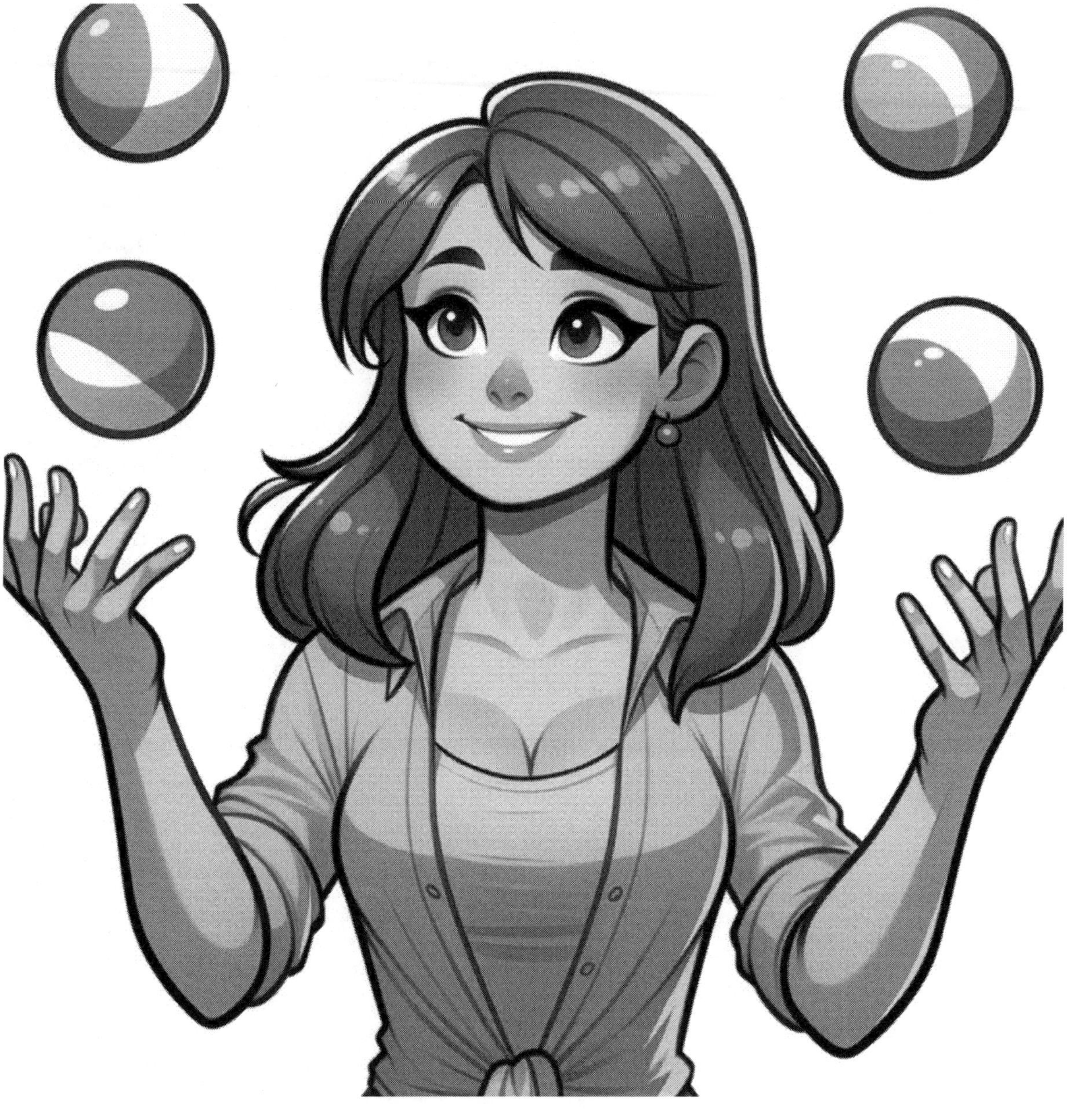

Tips for Practice

Consistent Arcs: Try to make your throws consistent in terms of height and distance. The balls should peak at the same height in the middle.

Steady Rhythm: Establish a steady rhythm. Counting out loud or mentally can help maintain this rhythm.

Eye Focus: Keep your eyes on the peak of the arc. This helps in timing your throws and catches.

Relaxed Posture: Stand comfortably with your feet shoulder-width apart and your elbows slightly bent. Avoid stiff or jerky movements.

One Throw at a Time: Focus on making one good throw and catch before moving on to the next. Don't rush into the second throw.

Practice Both Directions: Start with throwing from your dominant hand first, then practice starting with your non-dominant hand.

Common Challenges

Timing and Coordination: Getting the timing right between the throws and catches can be challenging. It takes practice to develop a smooth, coordinated rhythm.

Overthrowing: Beginners often tend to throw the balls too high or too far. Aim for controlled, gentle throws.

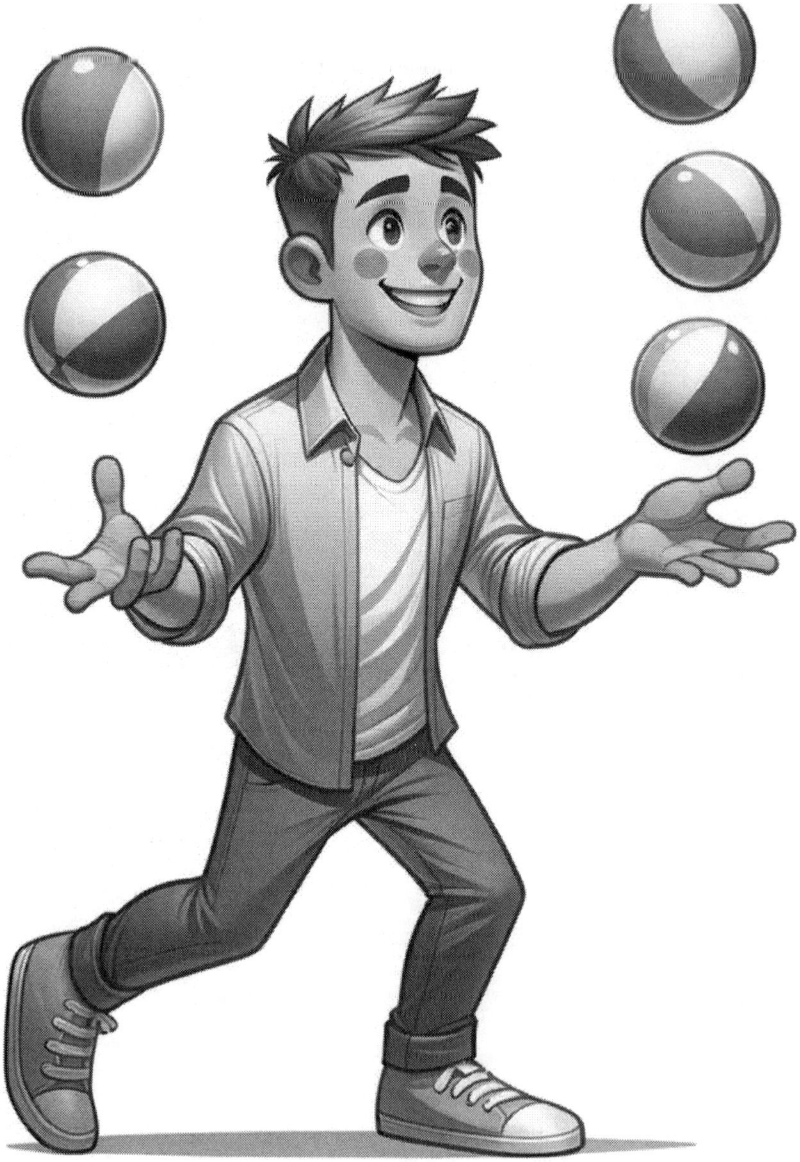

The Cascade is the most fundamental and widely recognized pattern in juggling, typically the first pattern learned by beginners. It involves juggling three balls in a continuous cycle, with each ball being thrown in an arc to the opposite hand. Here's how to learn and master the Three Ball Cascade:

Understanding the Three Ball Cascade

Objective: The goal is to keep three balls in constant motion, with each hand alternately throwing and catching a ball in a smooth, rhythmic pattern.

Technique:

Starting Position: Begin with two balls in your dominant hand and one ball in your non-dominant hand.

First Throw: Toss the first ball (from your dominant hand) in an arc to the opposite hand. The peak of the arc should be just above eye level, around the center of your body.

Second Throw: As the first ball reaches its peak and begins to descend, throw the second ball (from your non-dominant hand) underneath the first ball, towards your dominant hand, following a similar arc.

Catch and Continue: Catch the first ball with your non-dominant hand. As the second ball peaks and descends, throw the third ball (from your dominant hand) underneath the second ball towards your non-dominant hand.

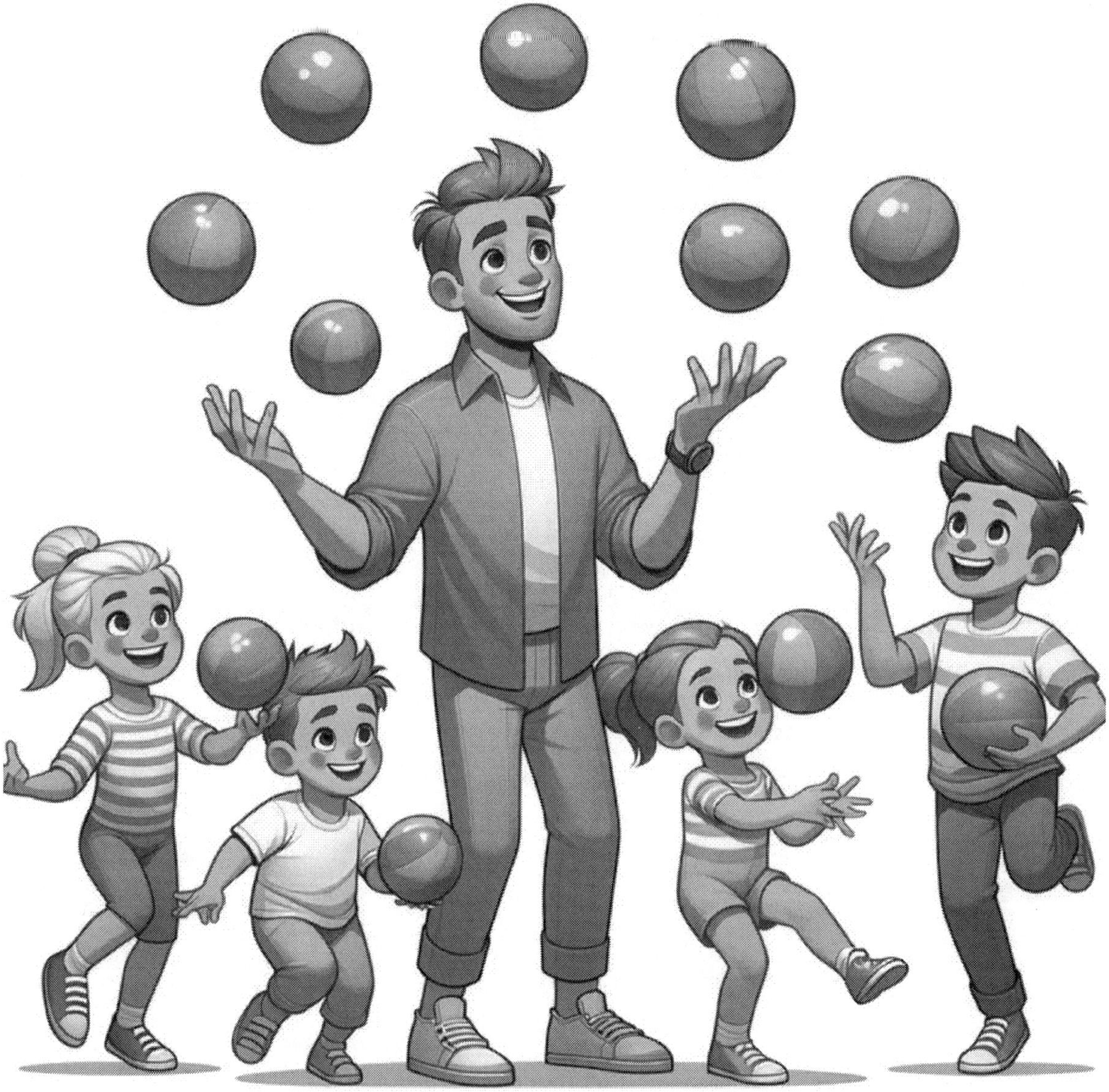

Tips for Practice

Consistent Throws: Focus on making your throws consistent in height and distance. Each ball should peak at the same point in the center.

Rhythm and Timing: Develop a steady rhythm. The cadence of the throws is crucial for maintaining the pattern.

Eye Focus: Keep your eyes on the apex of the throws. This helps in anticipating the catches.

Relaxed Posture: Maintain a relaxed stance with your elbows by your sides and your throws and catches at waist level.

Patience and Persistence: Learning the cascade takes time. Start slowly, and don't be discouraged by drops - they're a normal part of the learning process.

Practice in Steps: Break down the pattern. Start with one ball, move to two, and then progress to three.

Common Challenges

Asymmetrical Throws: Beginners often struggle with making their throws symmetrical. Practice with two balls to improve this.

Rushing the Pattern: Avoid rushing your throws. Take your time to establish a rhythm.

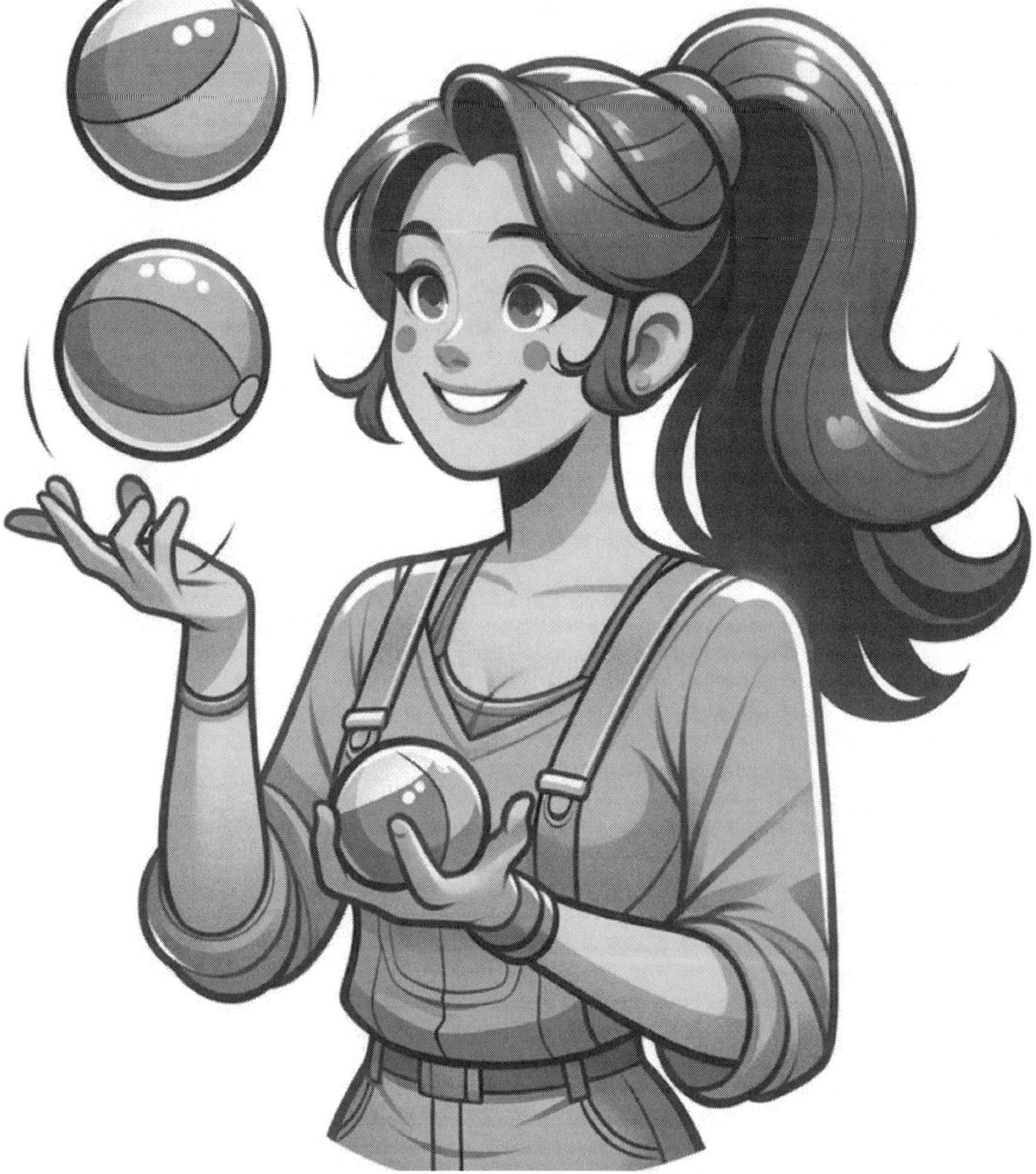

Embarking on the art of yo-yo juggling, one enters a world of skillful precision and rhythmic coordination.

The essence of Yo-Yo Juggling: The yo-yo, a pair of disks connected by an axle with a string wound around it, becomes an extension of the juggler's hand. The objective is to execute a series of tricks, each with its flair and complexity.

Technique:

Starting Position: Holding the yo-yo comfortably in one hand, the string is looped around the finger.

Basic Throw: The initial throw, key to setting the yo-yo into motion, requires a swift downward flick of the wrist.

Sleeping and Looping: 'Sleeping' involves the yo-yo spinning at the end of the string, while 'looping' is a rapid up-and-down movement.

String Tricks: Advanced maneuvers include creating patterns and landing the yo-yo on the string to form intricate shapes.

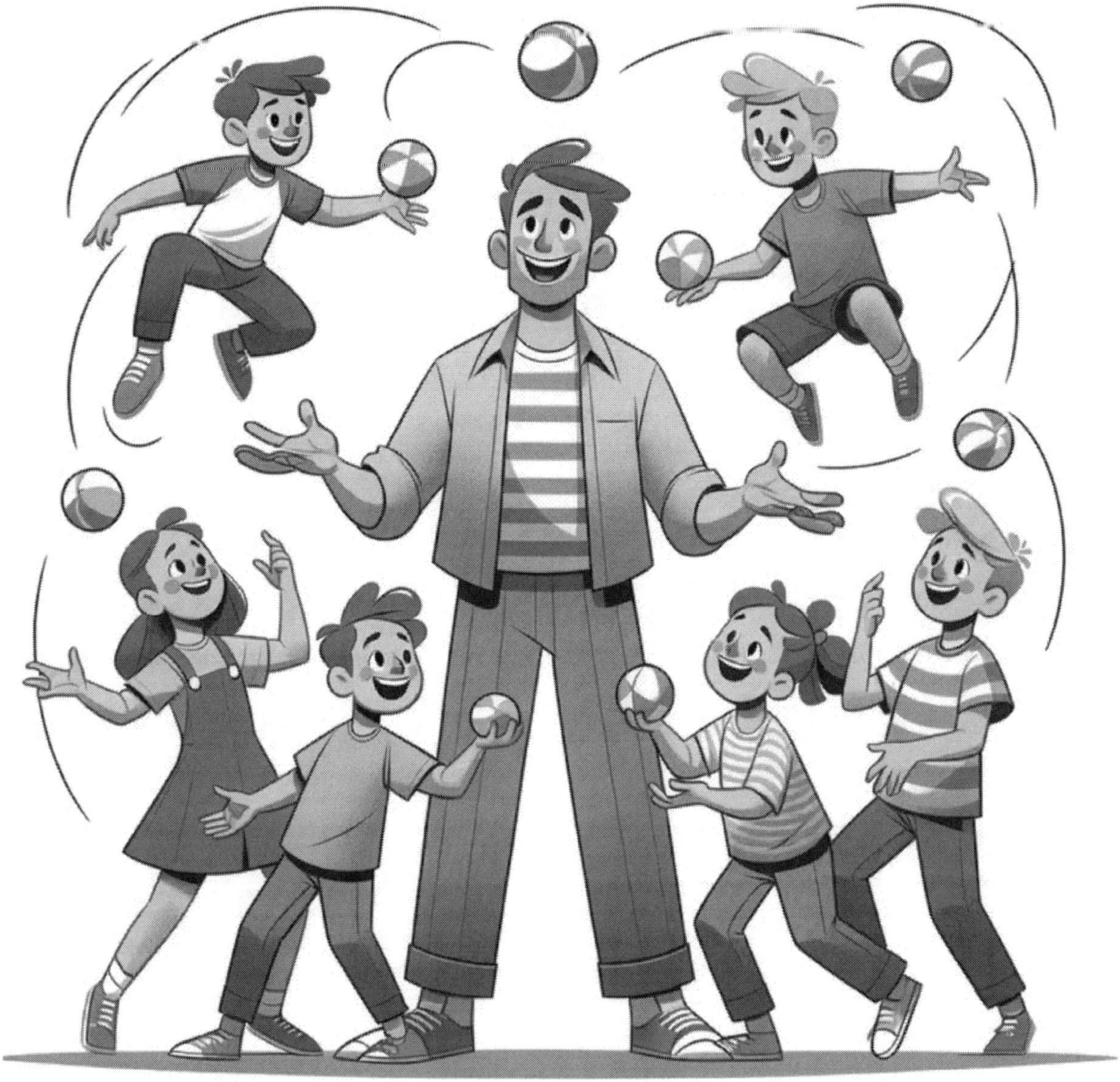

Importance in Juggling:

Skill Development: Yo-yo juggling honed fine motor skills and hand-eye coordination.

Rhythmic Coordination: The fluidity of movements demands a rhythmic synchronization between hand movements and the yo-yo's motion.

Creative Expression: Each trick and combination allows for personal expression and style.

Tips for Mastery:

Start Simple: Begin with basic throws and sleeping, gradually progressing to more complex tricks.

Consistent Practice: Regular practice is crucial for developing fluidity and precision.

Learn from Others: Watching tutorials or other yo-yo enthusiasts can provide new techniques and inspiration.

In essence, yo-yo juggling is a blend of physical skill, rhythm, and artistic expression, captivating both the performer and the audience with its dynamic and elegant movements.

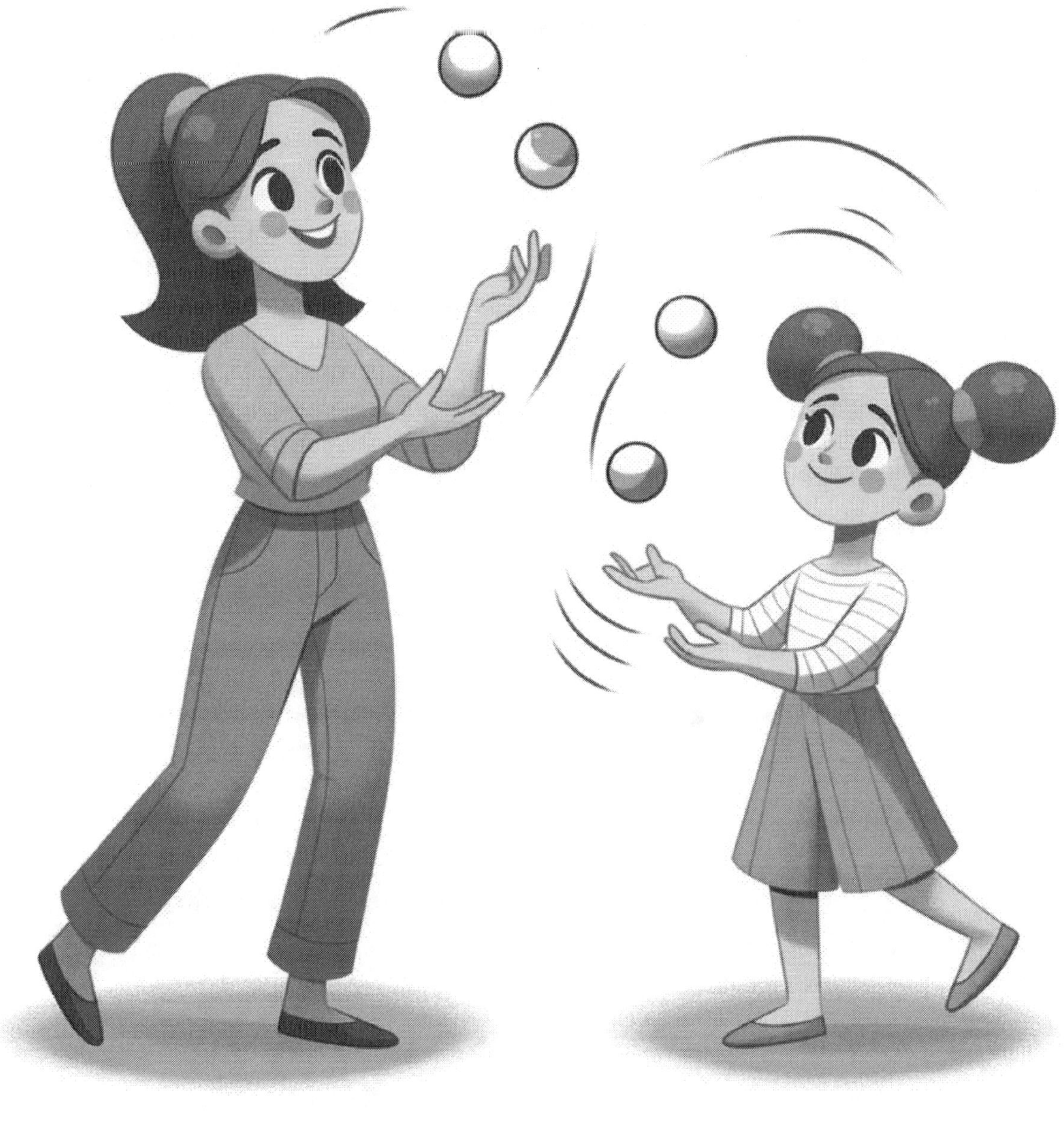

Embarking on the Rainbow Arches juggling style, one enters a realm of vibrant visual artistry and coordinated skill.

The essence of Rainbow Arches: This style involves the juggling of three balls in high, arching throws. Each ball soars in a sweeping motion, crossing paths in mid-air, akin to the arc of a rainbow. This pattern creates an overlapping and aesthetically pleasing effect.

Technique:

Starting Position: Holding three balls, begin with the standard cascade position.

High Throws: Each throw is made higher and in an outward arch, crossing over the other balls.

Continuous Motion: Maintain a fluid rhythm, ensuring each ball peaks and descends in a synchronized manner.

Importance in Juggling:

Enhanced Skill Level: Perfecting Rainbow Arches demands precise control and timing, elevating a juggler's skill.

Aesthetic Appeal: This style is visually captivating, adding a dynamic flair to juggling performances.

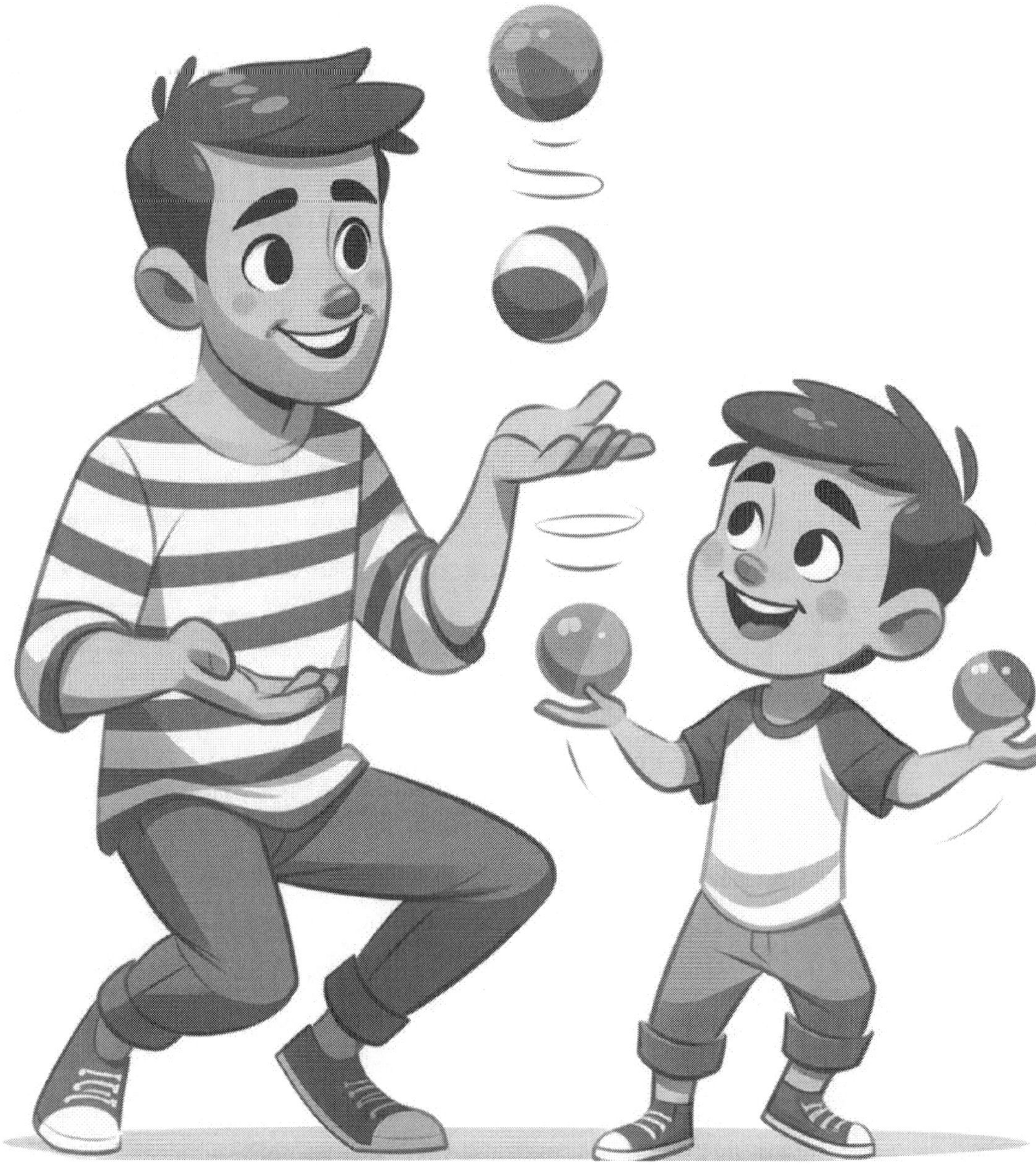

Building Timing Skills: Timing your clap and catch correctly is crucial and directly translates to better timing in more complex juggling patterns.

Increasing Difficulty Gradually: you can increase the difficulty by adding more claps, throwing higher, or even incorporating a second ball.

Tips for Effective Practice

Consistent Throws: Aim for consistent height and placement with your throws. This predictability makes the clap and catch easier.

Start Slow: Begin with a single, easy clap. As you get more comfortable, you can increase the speed or add more claps.

Keep Your Eyes on the Ball: Focus on the ball as you clap, ensuring you're ready to catch it as it comes down.

Relax and Have Fun: This exercise is meant to be fun and engaging. Stay relaxed and enjoy the challenge.

Rainbow Arches are not only a great training tool for aspiring jugglers but also a fun way to introduce a bit of flair and challenge into your juggling practice.

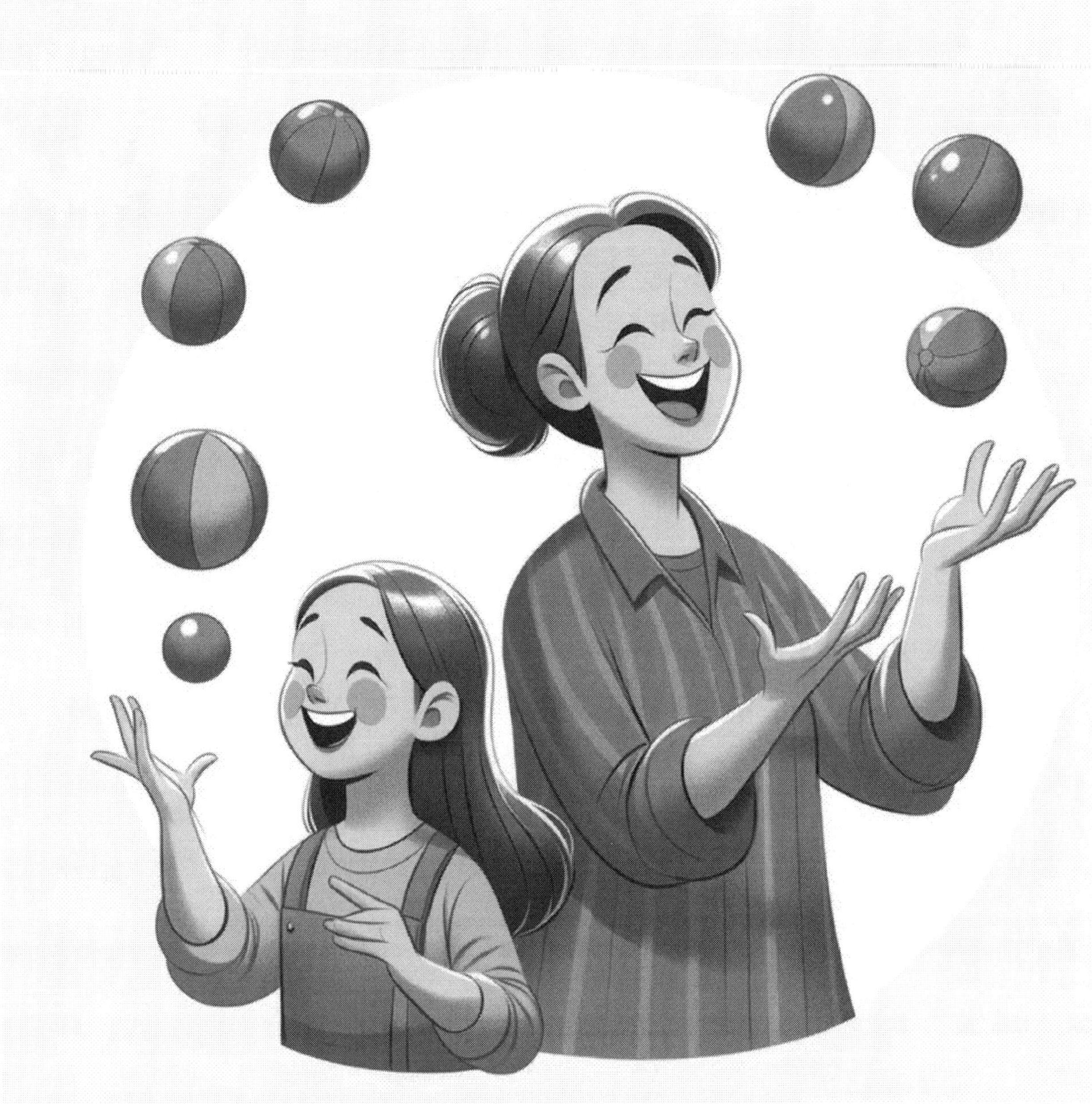

The Reverse Cascade is a fundamental juggling pattern, particularly appealing to those who have already mastered the basic three-ball cascade. It's a variation where the balls are thrown in a reverse pattern, creating a visually striking effect. Here's an overview of the Reverse Cascade:

Understanding the Reverse Cascade

Objective: In the Reverse Cascade, instead of throwing the balls in an underhand arc (as in the regular cascade), you throw them overhand. This means the balls are tossed over the top in an outward motion, creating an arc that is visually the opposite of the standard cascade.

Technique:

Starting Position: Begin with the same setup as the regular three-ball cascade – two balls in one hand and one in the other.

First Throw: Toss the first ball in an overhand motion, so it peaks above eye level and slightly outward.

Continuing the Pattern: As the first ball begins to descend, throw the second ball from your other hand in the same manner, so it arcs over the first ball.

Maintaining the Pattern: Continue alternating your throws in this overhand, outward arcing motion. The balls should follow a pattern that looks like an inverted U shape.

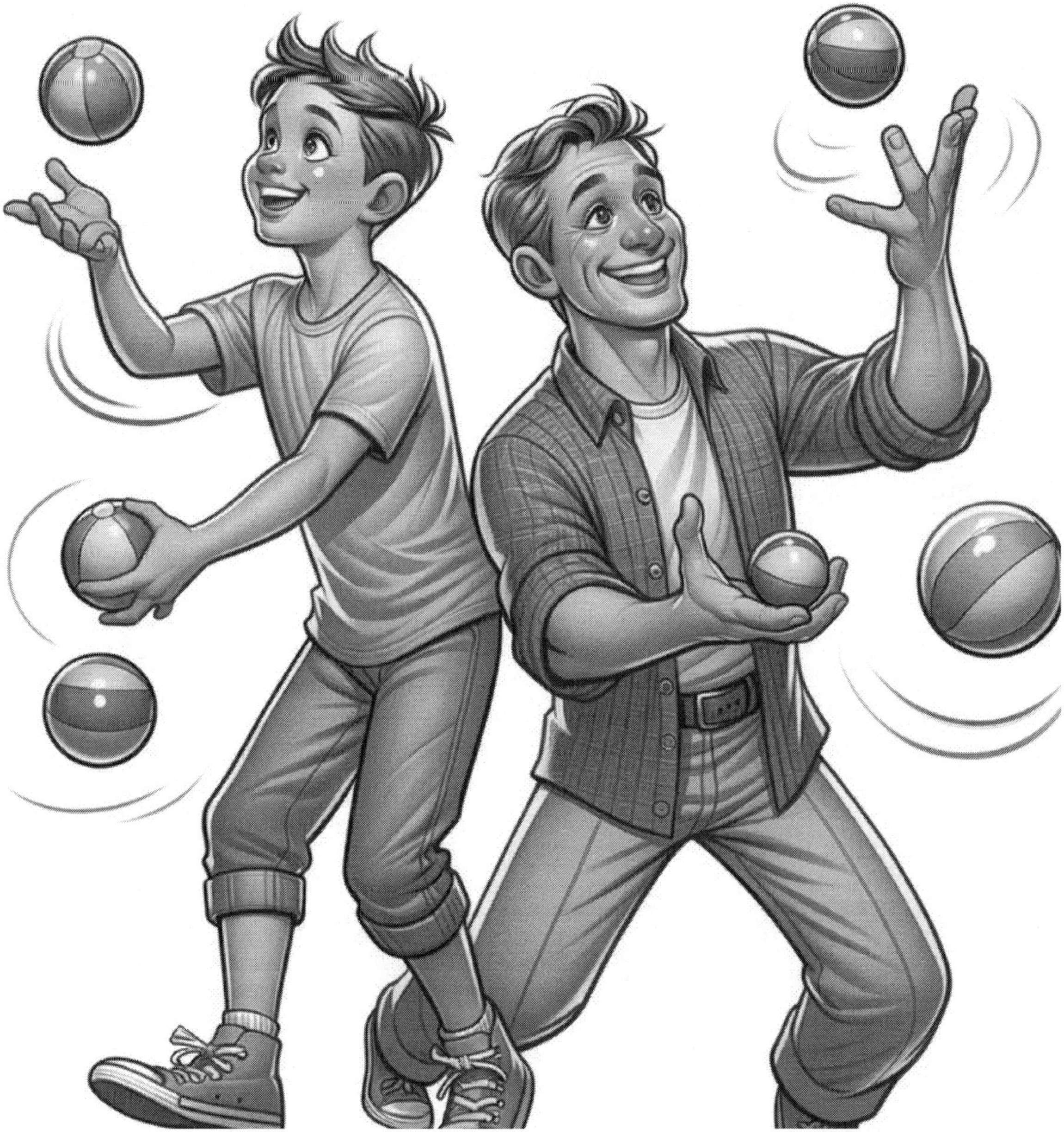

Importance in Juggling

Skill Development: The Reverse Cascade helps develop a higher skill level in juggling by introducing a new throwing motion and rhythm.

Enhanced Coordination and Timing: This pattern requires more precise timing and coordination, as the throws and catches are in a less natural motion compared to the regular cascade.

Visual Appeal: It offers a different visual effect, adding variety to your juggling repertoire.

Tips for Effective Practice

Master the Regular Cascade First: It's essential to be comfortable with the standard cascade before attempting the reverse version.

Focus on Throw Arcs: Pay attention to the arcs of your throws. They should be even and consistent.

Start Slowly: Begin by practicing the motion with one ball, then two, before attempting three.

Watch the Peaks: As with the regular cascade, your focus should be on the peak of the throws.

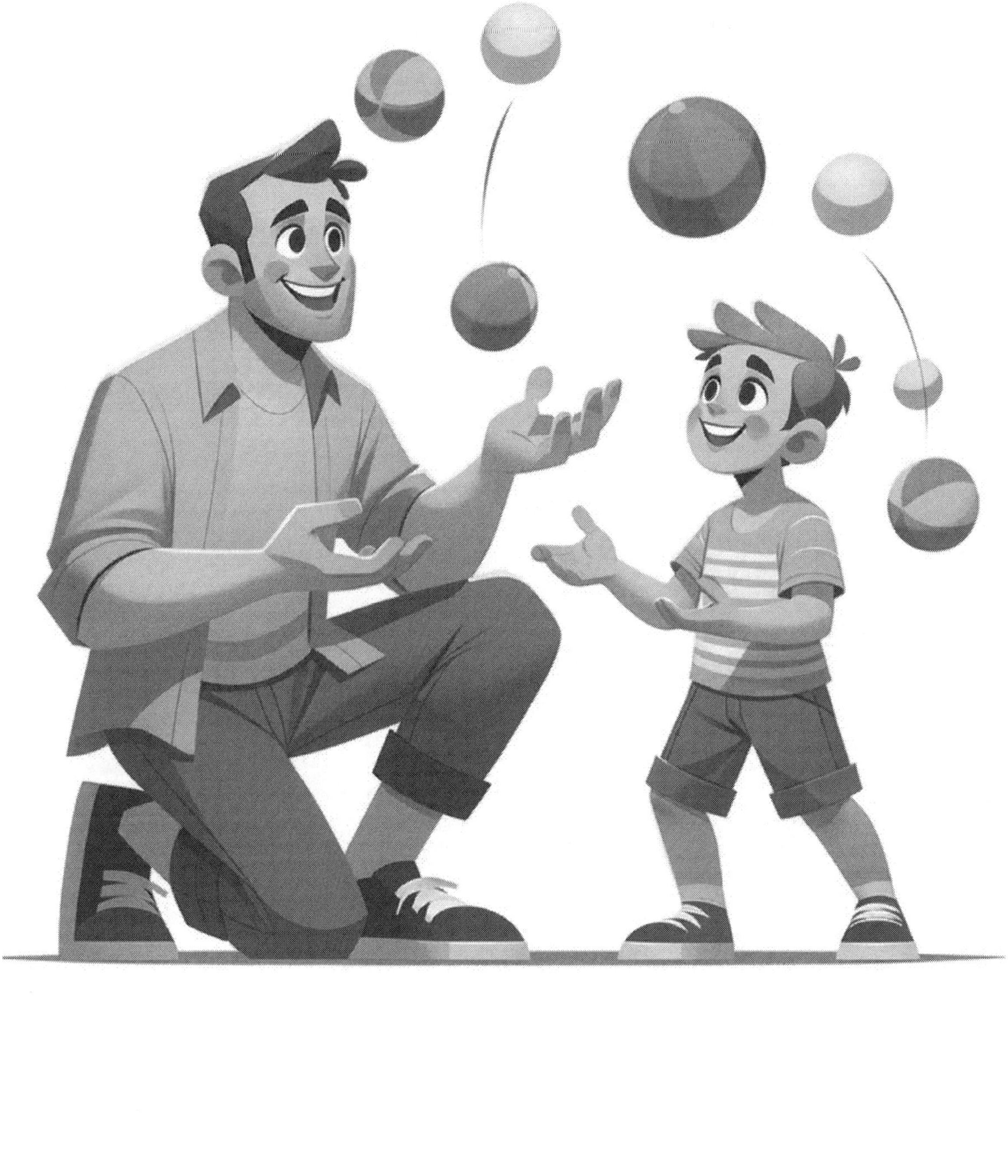

Columns is a distinctive juggling pattern that is particularly appealing for its structured, visually pleasing form. It's often recommended for jugglers who have a grasp of the basic cascade and are looking to add variety to their repertoire. Here's a detailed look at Columns:

Understanding Columns

Objective: In the Columns pattern, instead of throwing the balls in a crossing pattern (like in the cascade), each ball is thrown and caught in vertical lines, or "columns." This pattern can be performed with two or three balls.

Technique:

Starting Position: Begin with two or three balls. If using three, start with two in one hand and one in the other.

Basic Two-Ball Columns: Start with one ball in each hand. Throw one ball up in a straight line and, as it comes down, throw the other ball up in a parallel line next to it. Catch each ball in the same hand that threw it. The balls move up and down in two distinct columns.

Three-Ball Columns: With three balls, you'll throw the two balls in your dominant hand up in two outer columns, while the ball in your non-dominant hand goes up and down in the middle column. The outer balls are thrown and caught by the same hand, while the middle ball is passed back and forth between hands.

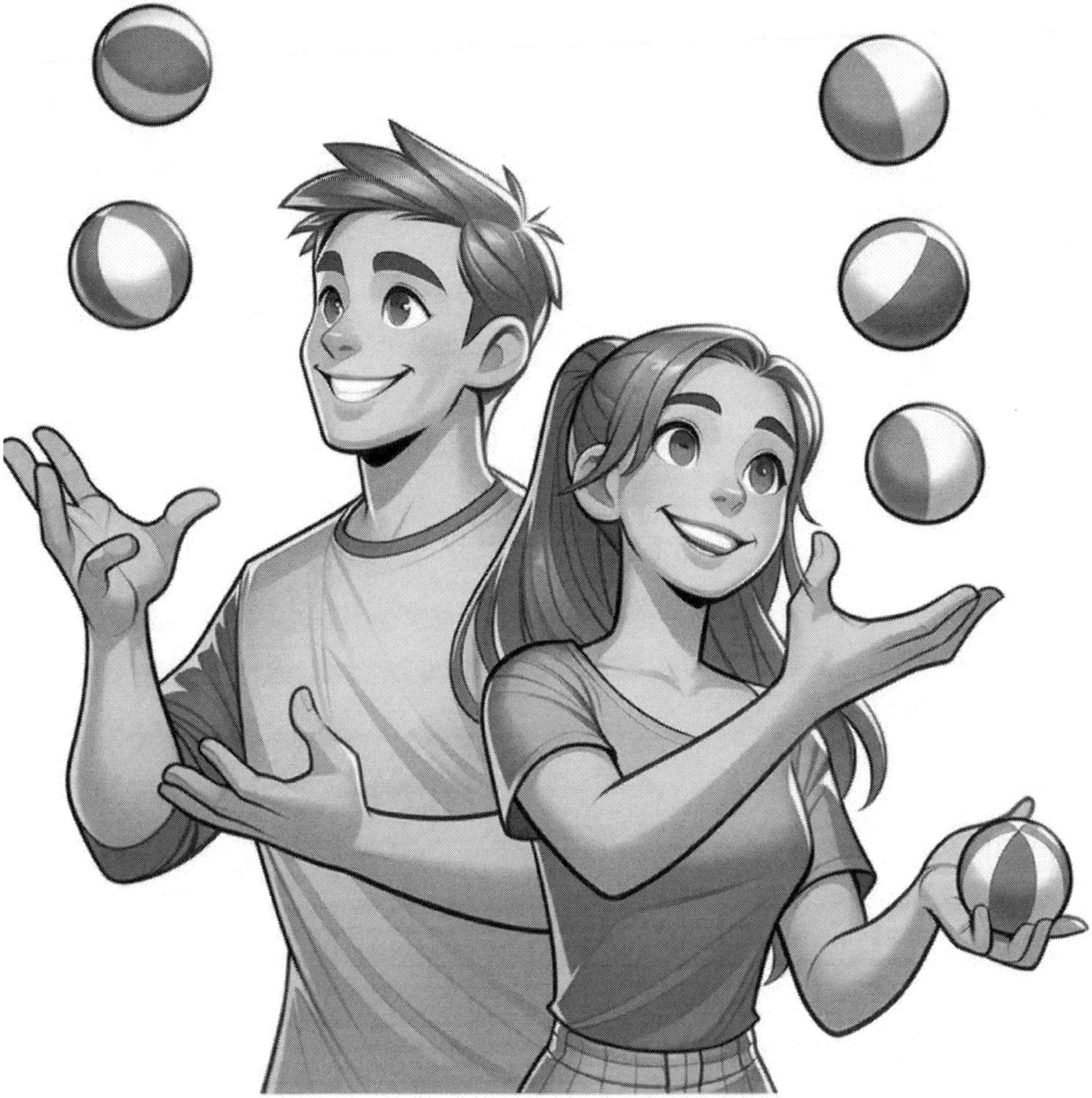

Importance in Juggling

Skill Variation: Columns introduce a different skill set from the cascade, focusing on vertical, synchronized throws.

Hand Independence: This pattern helps develop independence between your hands, as each hand is responsible for its own column.

Visual Effect: Columns have a distinct look, adding a visually appealing and rhythmic pattern to your juggling.

Tips for Effective Practice

Even Throws: Aim to keep your throws at the same height and speed for consistency.
Hand Movement: Minimize sideways hand movement. The pattern relies on vertical throws.

Focus on the Peaks: Keep your eyes on the top of the columns to better time your catches and throws.

Start with Two Balls: Get comfortable with two-ball columns before adding the third ball.

Practice Both Hands: Ensure both hands are equally practiced, especially if using the three-ball variation.

.

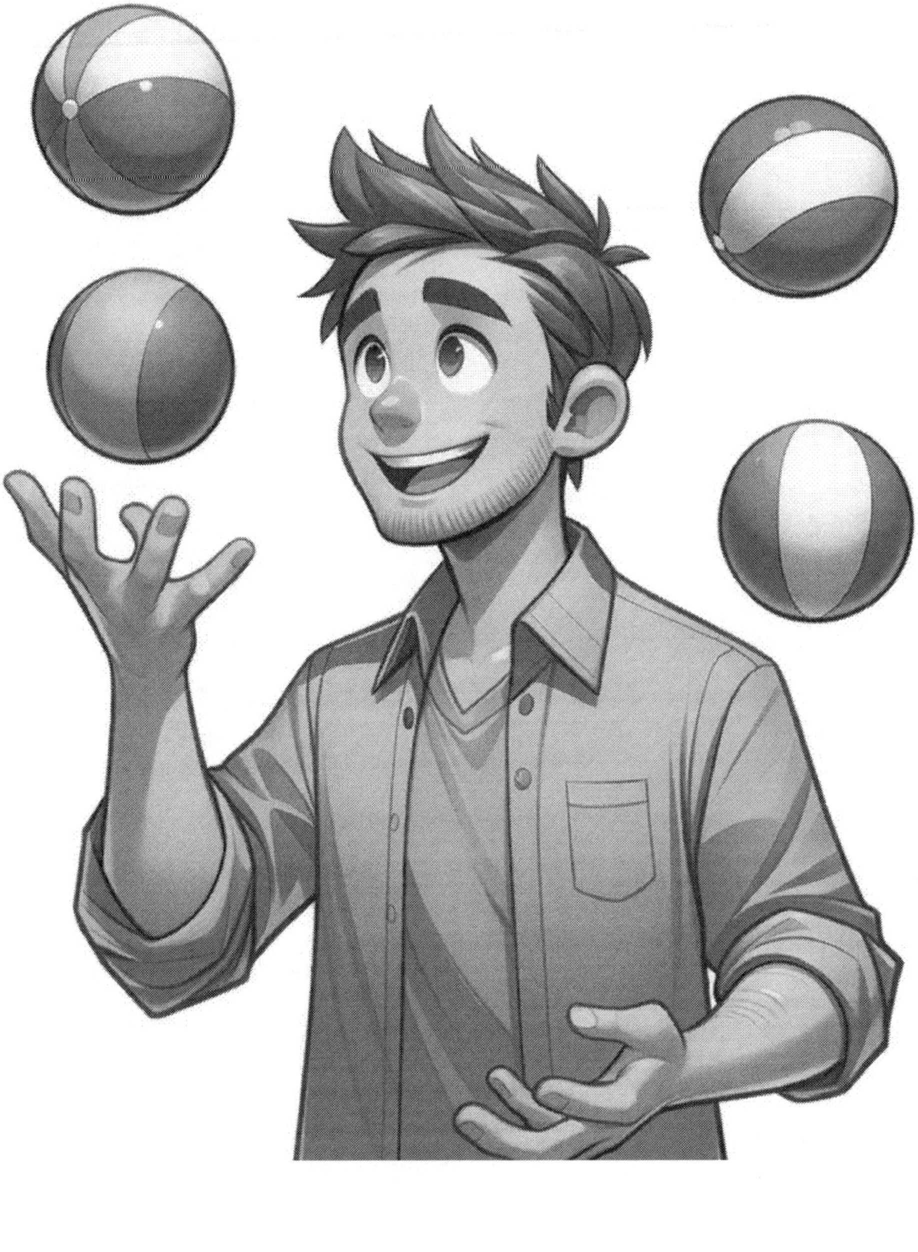

The Half Shower is a classic juggling pattern that adds variety and a new level of complexity to the basic three-ball cascade. It's an asymmetric pattern where balls are thrown over the top in one direction and underneath in the opposite direction. Here's a closer look at how to perform the Half Shower:

Understanding the Half Shower

Objective: The objective is to create a pattern where one hand always throws the balls over the top (in a higher arc), and the other hand throws them back underneath in a lower arc.

Technique:

Starting Position: Begin with two balls in your dominant hand and one in your non-dominant hand, similar to the starting position for a three-ball cascade.

Throwing Pattern: Start with a standard cascade throw. As the ball peaks and starts to descend, make an over-the-top throw with your dominant hand. This throw should be higher and more outward than the cascade throw.

Catching and Continuing: Catch the first ball with your non-dominant hand. As it comes down, make a lower, more direct throwback to your dominant hand. This creates a cycle where the dominant hand is always making the higher throw.

Maintaining the Pattern: Continue this pattern, with the balls creating a semi-circular path – up and over from the dominant hand, then straight back underneath from the non-dominant hand.

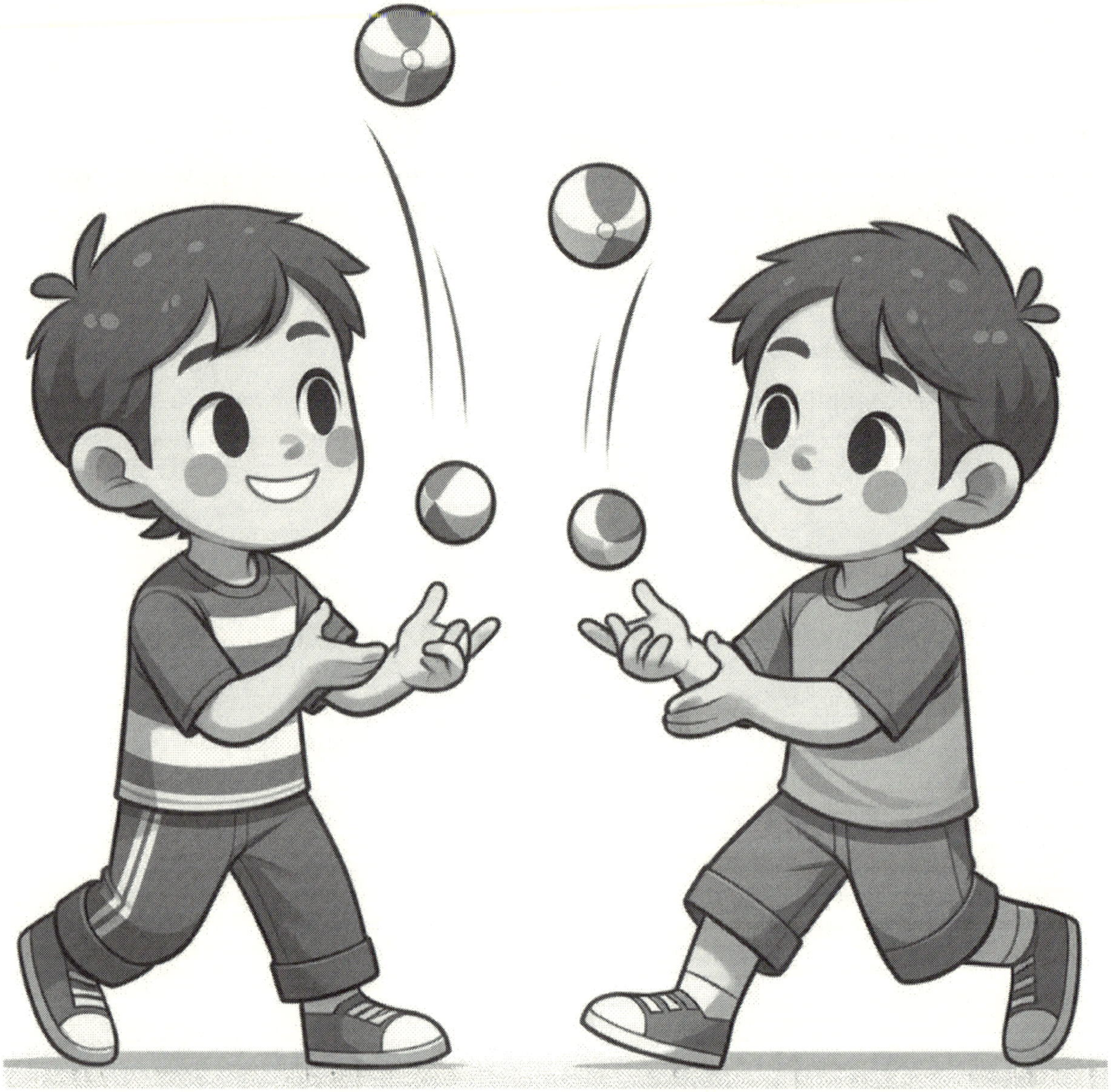

Importance in Juggling

Skill Advancement: The Half Shower is a step up from the basic cascade and is excellent for developing more advanced juggling skills.

Hand Coordination: It enhances hand coordination, as each hand has a distinct role in the pattern.

Rhythm and Timing: This pattern helps develop a sense of rhythm and timing, as the throws are asymmetrical yet need to be coordinated smoothly.

Tips for Effective Practice

Consistent Over-the-Top Throws: Focus on making the over-the-top throws consistent in height and arc.

Steady Lower Throws: Ensure the lower throws are steady and controlled, providing a stable rhythm to the pattern.

Focus on Both Hands: Pay equal attention to both hands, as each has a specific and crucial role in the pattern.

Start Slowly: Begin practicing slowly and increase speed as you become more comfortable.

Visual Focus: Keep your eyes focused on the peak of the higher throws to better time your catches and subsequent throws.

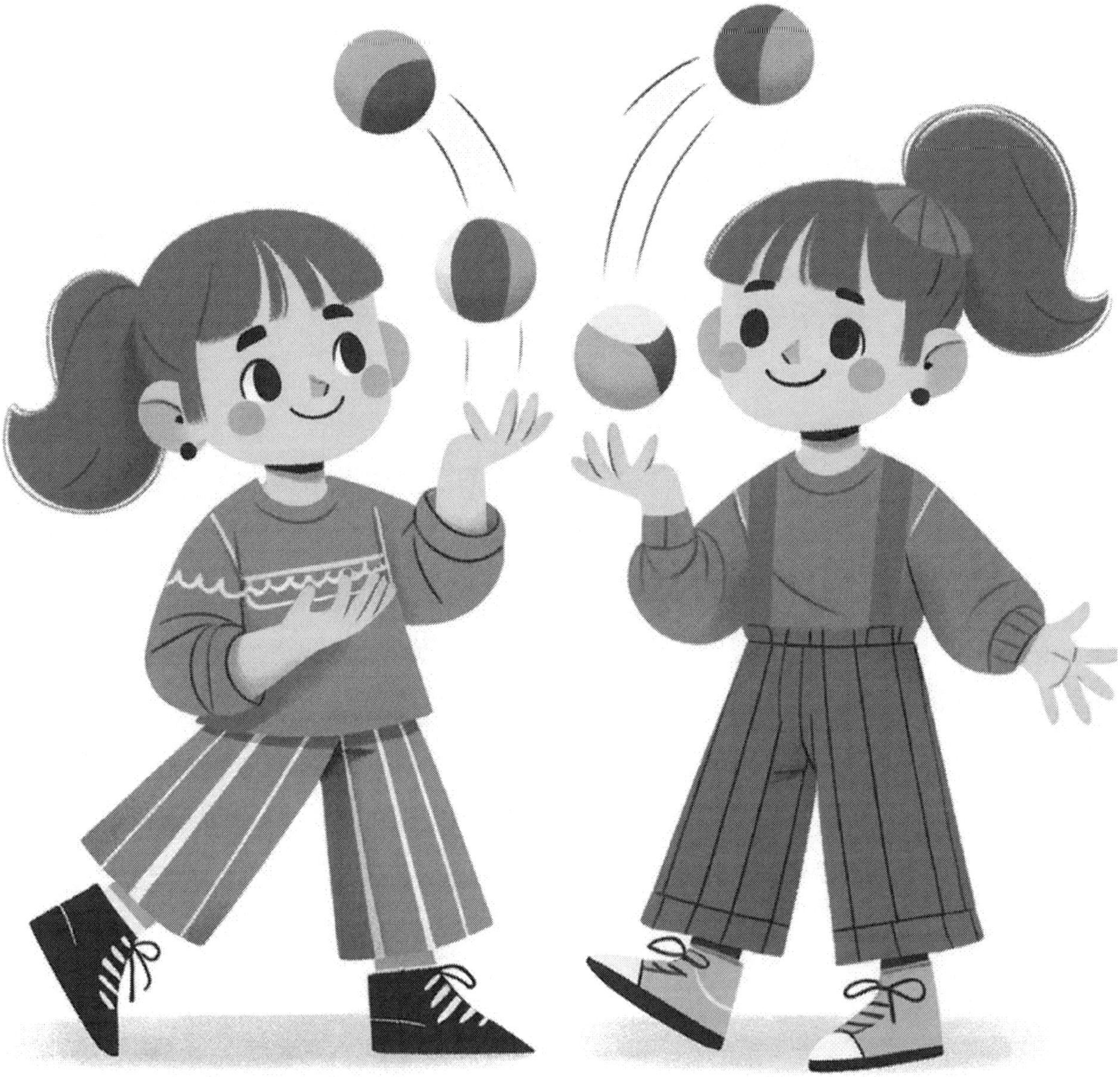

The Factory juggling style is a unique and structured pattern that emulates the movements of a mechanical assembly line, often using three balls:

Technique: In this style, two balls are juggled in a circular pattern in one hand, while the third ball is shuttled back and forth above them in a straight line, mimicking a conveyor belt.

Visual Appeal: The Factory creates a mechanical illusion, as if the balls are components being moved along a production line.

Skill Enhancement: This pattern challenges and develops a juggler's coordination, timing, and ability to multitask.

Mastering the Factory:

Begin with Two Balls: Practice the circular motion in one hand with two balls.

Introduce the Third Ball: Add the third ball, focusing on the linear movement and its timing with the circular pattern.

Maintain Rhythm: Keep a consistent, machine-like rhythm to ensure the fluidity of the pattern.

In essence, the Factory style is a mesmerizing mix of rhythm, precision, and mechanical mimicry, adding a unique flavor to the juggling repertoire.

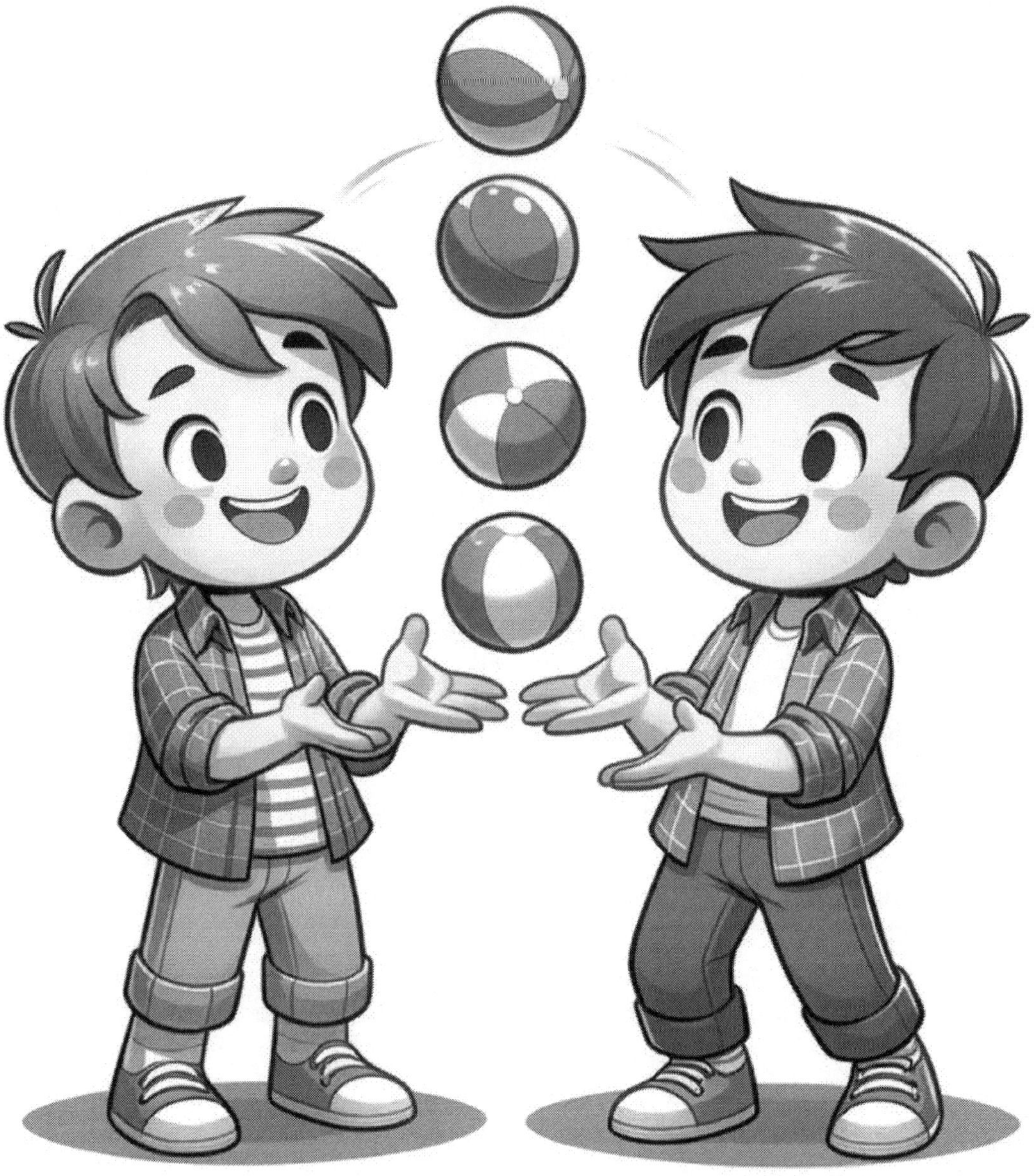

Importance in Juggling

Variation in Skill: Factory introduces a variation in throw heights and adds a visual twist to the standard cascade.

Focus and Timing: This pattern requires focus and timing to maintain the cascade while integrating the high-arcing throws.

Hand Coordination: It enhances hand coordination as one ball follows a different path, requiring careful control.

Tips for Effective Practice

Consistent High Throws: Make sure the high throws are consistent in height and arc.

Smooth Cascade Underneath: Keep the cascade pattern smooth and steady with the other two balls.

Timing of Throws: Work on the timing of the high throw so that it integrates seamlessly into the cascade.

Practice Both Directions: Practice making the high throw with both hands to develop symmetry in your skills.

Visual Tracking: Keep an eye on the high throw while managing the cascade, which can be challenging initially.

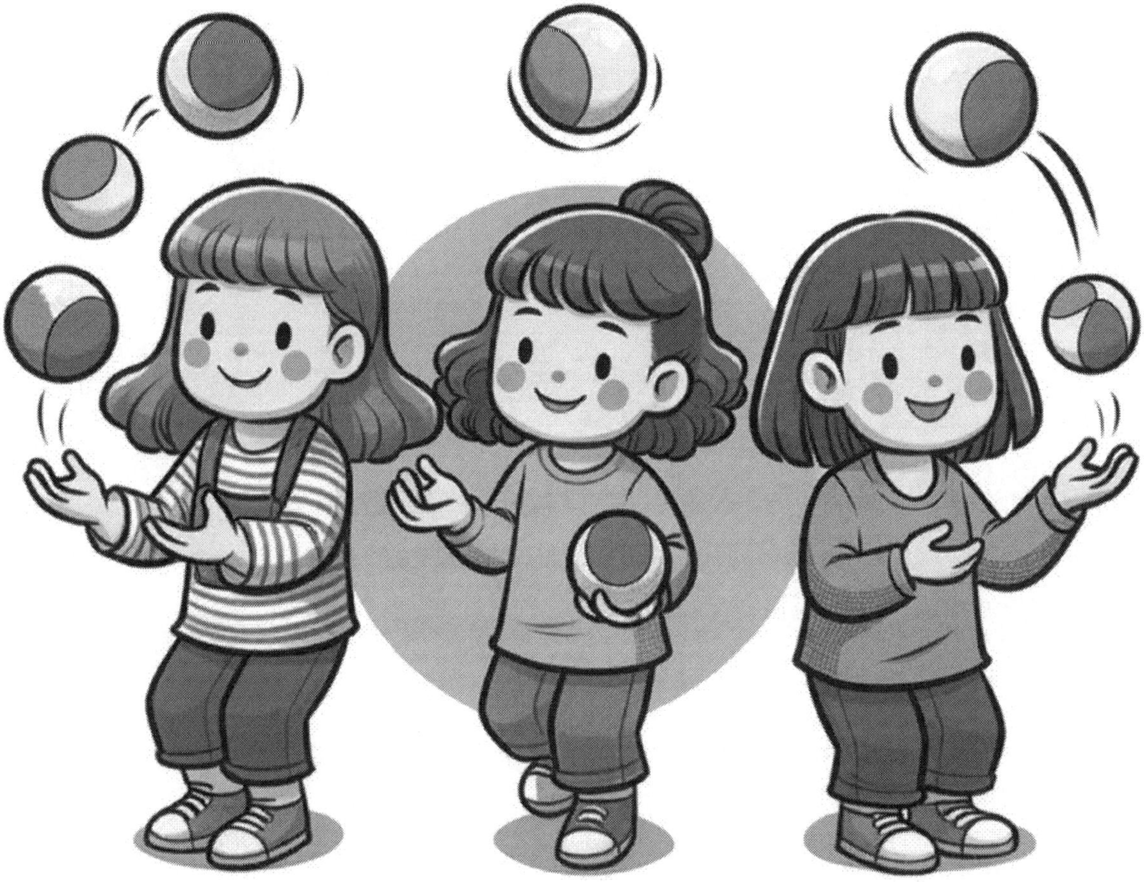

Embarking on Juggler's Tennis, one delves into a rhythmic and playful juggling pattern that mimics the motion of a tennis match:

The essence of Juggler's Tennis: This style involves alternating throws in a standard three-ball cascade, where one ball (the 'tennis ball') is arched over the others in a distinct path, resembling a tennis ball being hit over a net.

Technique:

Starting Position: Begin with the regular three-ball cascade.

Tennis Ball Throw: One ball is thrown in a higher arch over the top, crossing above the other two balls in a regular cascade pattern.

Alternating Pattern: The high arching ball switches sides each time, creating a visual effect of a tennis match.

Importance in Juggling:

Skill Development: Juggler's Tennis enhances control and precision, adding variety to the juggler's skills.

Visual Interest: This style is engaging and adds a playful element to juggling routines.

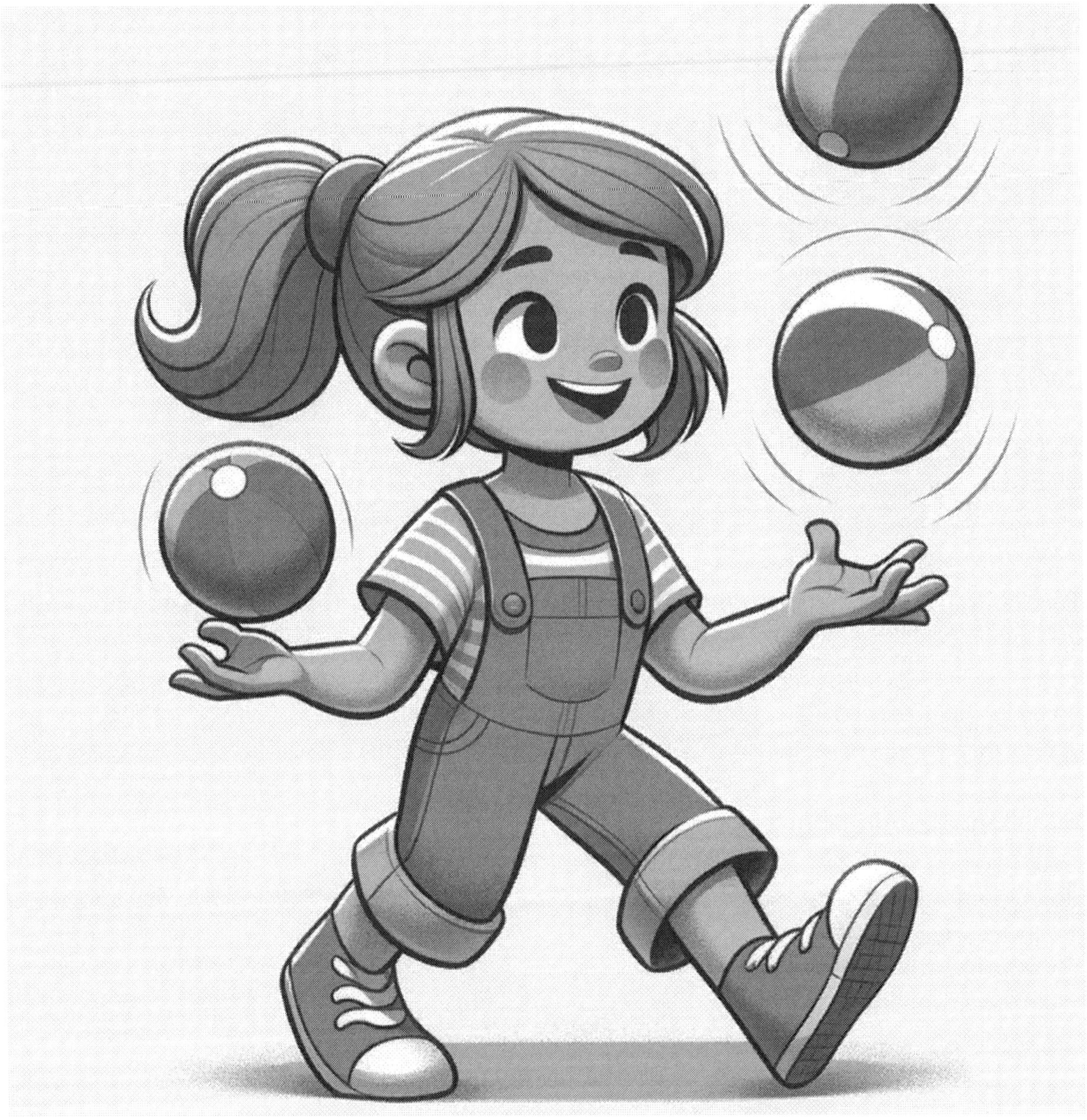

Importance in Juggling

Enhanced Coordination: Jugglers Tennis requires a higher level of hand-eye coordination, as you need to manage the throws and catches while crossing and uncrossing your arms.

Improved Dexterity: This pattern challenges your dexterity and agility, making it a great exercise to enhance your juggling skills.

Visual Appeal: Jugglers Tennis adds a dramatic and entertaining element to juggling, making the performance more visually interesting.

Tips for Effective Practice

Start Slowly: Begin with slower throws to give yourself time to cross and uncross your arms.

Maintain Rhythm: Try to keep a consistent rhythm, even with the added complexity of crossing arms.

Practice One Arm at a Time: Initially, practice arm crosses with throws from just one hand before alternating.

Focus on Fluid Motion: Aim for smooth and fluid arm movements to make the pattern look more graceful.

Keep Throws Controlled: Ensure your throws aren't too wide or erratic, as this makes arm crosses more difficult.

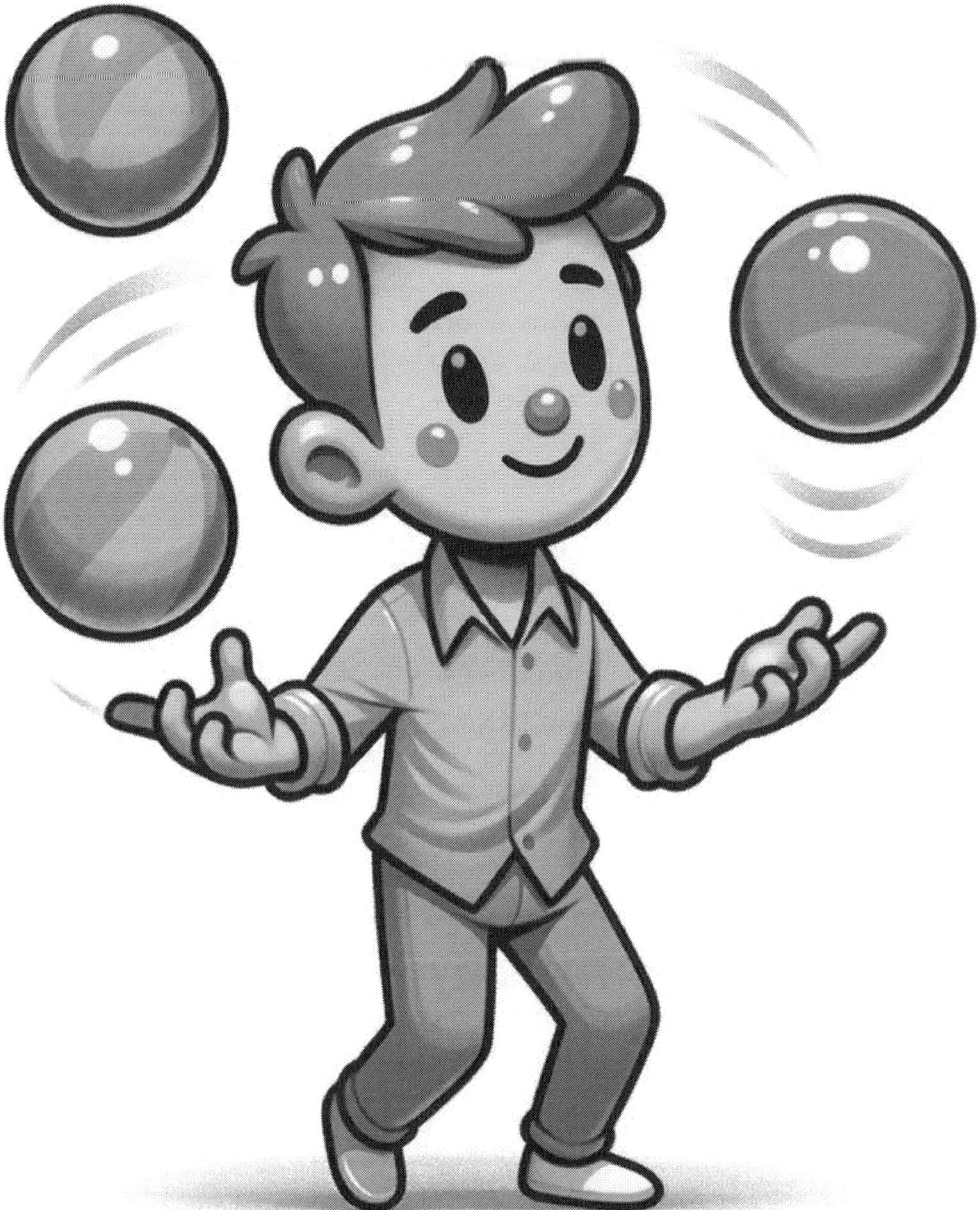

Visualization of Juggling Styles Suitable for Beginners

| Jugglers Tennis | Half-Shower | Cascade | Reverse Cascade |

| Yo-Yo | Rainbow Arches | Factory | Column |

Afterword

As we reach the end of "Juggling for Beginners," it's important to reflect on the journey we've embarked on together. Juggling is not just a skill; it's an art form that combines physical coordination, mental discipline, and creative expression. Through the pages of this book, you've been introduced to the fundamentals of juggling, starting from the very basics to more intricate patterns and techniques.

Remember, the path to becoming a proficient juggler is as unique as the individual. It's a journey filled with dropped balls, unexpected catches, and moments of triumph. Each page of this book was designed not just to teach you the mechanics of juggling but to also instill a sense of patience and persistence – qualities that are invaluable in juggling and in life.

Juggling is a metaphor for balance and rhythm, for throwing and catching, for learning and growing. The skills you develop through juggling – focus, coordination, and timing – are skills that can enhance other areas of your life. Juggling teaches us to embrace our mistakes as learning opportunities and to celebrate our successes, no matter how small. As you move forward, keep in mind that practice is key. The more you juggle, the more you'll understand the subtle nuances of the art. Don't be discouraged by initial challenges; they are stepping stones to your success. Share your juggling journey with others, learn from fellow jugglers, and become a part of the vibrant juggling community. Finally, remember to have fun. The joy of juggling comes not just from mastering a pattern but from the process of learning and growing. Whether you juggle for relaxation, for performance, or as a way to challenge yourself, keep the joy in your juggling.

Made in the USA
Las Vegas, NV
26 May 2024